the world revisited

A TRAVEL BOOK WITH DRAWINGS

BY STEPHEN LONGSTREET

Decade
Land I Live
Stallion Road
Sound of an American
The Jolson Story
High Button Shoes
Last Man Around the World
Three Days
The Pedlocks
The Beach House

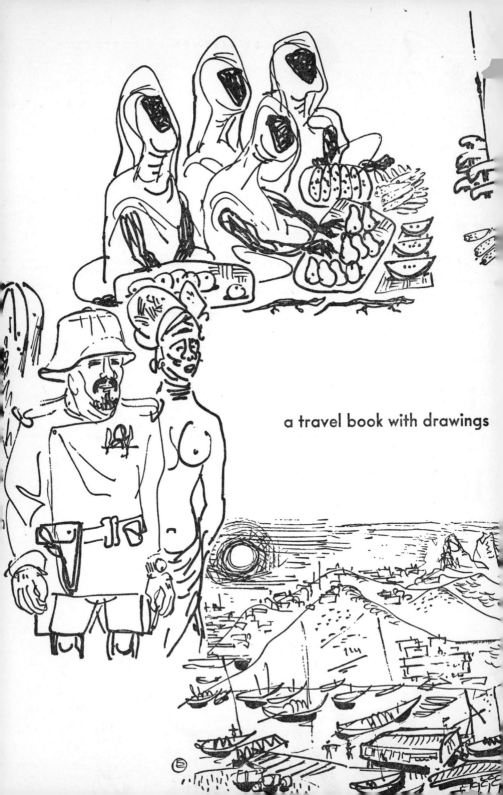

a travel book with drawings

Stephen Longstreet

THE WORLD
REVISITED

HENRY HOLT AND COMPANY
NEW YORK

THERE IS NOTHING WORSE FOR MORTALS THAN A WANDERING LIFE—HOMER: Odyssey

FOR

Zeal and
Energy in
The free press

a word before

THE USE OF TRAVEL IS TO REGULATE IMAGINATION BY REAL-
ITY, AND INSTEAD OF THINKING HOW THINGS MAY BE, TO
SEE THEM AS THEY ARE . . .
SAMUEL JOHNSON

THERE was once a travel book called *Last Man Around the World,* and I wrote it about a dozen years ago. I thought at the time that no one could again go around the world just for pleasure in time and space, just for the looking at things and people. It was the last trip of the white luxury liner (three kinds of hot breads) before they made her into a troop carrier. A German U-boat sank her in the cold of a North Atlantic dawn, and down to the bottom with her went a lot of a world and a great deal of the charm of a young man's idea of things.

But now I have again been around the world, older but not in any way wiser, and in no form any more alert to the signs and the noises that I could interpret as to what the future will be. I can't even read palms.

II

I don't know what kind of travel book this is, but I do know what kind it *isn't*. It is not the book of an easy expert on international affairs, of a jet-propelled broom under a journalist with a crystal ball in every pocket. Here are no studies of economics, tonnage, crops, political systems, or predictions of daffier creeds, cultures, or tomorrow's headlines. This book is frankly the by-product of an earnest painter, a novelist, and a passable human being in his middle years, visiting again the places he once knew, and some he really once loved. Their façades have changed, but so has the traveler, my mirror tells me. The sun, however, shines just as bright and the people look about life-size (I found no "little people"—they were all about my build) ; the only thing inflated was the money, some of our hopes, and the egos of the heroes of our times who seem to forget they are mortal. There are no dramatic peeps behind iron or even nylon curtains, no material here ready to be cut up into spy thrillers. No lamenting either at a portable wailing wall, nor too much brooding in a very beautiful and foolish world.

III

I write of the atmosphere around me and the things that glitter and frankly color my time on earth. If some of it seems trivial, and some of it full of talk of art and women and food and the landscapes, this is the way *I* see the world. Its faults are there, its pleasures wide and handsome. The stink and the reek of the world is here, too, I know; and the lean and hungry, the crippled and the depraved, appear around its smoldering edges. I have made no attempt to edit the world (I wish it would act the same toward me), and so for good or bad it's all here, or as much as I could cram into these journals, kept not too faithfully or in much detail, and in these drawings of things seen and touched.

IV

This is a book of the just-gone past, and therefore its people are living people. Not to harm them I have changed names (and even places, reworked dates) because most of them were kind, and I do not want to hurt anyone, or someone, that the novelist's nose and finger have set down a little closer to life than is expected if this were just journalism. Always remember, this is the book of a writer of novels and painter of pictures, and my interest has not always been in the sleek surface, the glib reporting of people and events to meet a date line. I have cut a great deal, added very little.

There are no State Department secrets here, no information that would be of value to any enemy, nothing to cause international double talk; in this world I remain a friendly witness. It is the world of my favorite poet, Andrew Marvell, who wrote:

THE WORLD IN ALL DOTH BUT TWO NATIONS BEAR,
THE GOOD AND THE BAD, AND THESE MIX EVERYWHERE . . .

So if there is a moral in this book, the only one I know of is printed above.

Stephen Longstreet

PEOPLE ARE PEOPLE

contents

book 1

ONCE MORE THE BIG APPLE

CALIFORNIA LANDSCAPE

1   traveler in mothballs

MOST world travelers prepare for their trips. Mine seem to spring suddenly on me and before I can let the milkman know to stop delivery of two quarts of Grade A and a pint of cream (I often wonder who drinks the stuff—I don't), I'm having my passport fingered. . . . One night my phone rang and a voice with an Old School Tie range of tones, that had seen Eton and Oxford plain, said:

"How are you, Old Hoss?"

"Hello?" I answered.

"Are you there?" replied the voice in London tones.

MY FRIEND TURTLE

I said I was and the voice cleared its throat and paused just long enough, I was sure, to insert a scotch-and-splash under its Guardsman's mustache.

"I say, Old Hoss, it's Turtle. I'm here to get you to agree to go around the world."

"I've already done it."

"Always do things by twos or sixes. I say, you do remember me?"

MY FRIEND TURTLE

Of course I remembered Turtle. He was really known by another name, but all his close friends called him Turtle. He

ran one of those English motion picture studios that were all
a deliberate exodus from sanity. They sent cameramen in
leather pants to climb a mountain in India, or to cross a river
someplace no one needed a river crossed, or to go to Mecca
(for some reason English journalism thinks nothing more
exciting than joining a caravan on its way to Mecca). It was
all good, solid stuff—and I liked the movies they made.

"How's England?" I asked.

"Foggy, when I left."

"How are politics?"

"The same. How about the trip to take colored travel stuff
for one of our films? We'll pay your expenses. How does it
sound?"

"Sounds for a younger man."

"Nonsense. I'll take you to dinner and we'll settle it."

I said I couldn't go. I was big with a new novel and the
labor pains were already starting. It was a book I had been
planning to do for a long time, and it was almost ready to
type itself. But Turtle said I could finish it in Turkey or India
or Nice. I said that I would meet him at Chasen's for dinner
and that he didn't have to dress, as we were only goddamn
Colonials and didn't have the refined habits of the English.
And he said, "You still have an overripe mind, like a cheese
gone too strong."

"Thanks."

Turtle, when I met him, was looking balder and thinner,
and his shoulders were a little rounder. He held his scotch-
and-splash a little tighter, but otherwise he was the same old
Turtle, a bored, earnest craftsman, a keen but worried man.
He was even making a lot of money, but it was being taxed
away. He didn't mind, as he said, "Because, Old Hoss, I have
a ringside seat on the fall of an Empire. Didn't you ever wish
while reading Gibbon that you might have been there to see
the old Roman Empire totter?"

"That's not very noble," I said. "You ought to want the Empire clear-eyed and bushy-tailed again."

"Oh, I'm a realist. You can't stop the pattern of history. If the age of Dickens, and floggings to death in the fleet, and the old-fashioned Christmas, and Shakespeare, and the noble prose of Shelley and Byron is to go, well, let it go."

"The last two were poets."

Turtle grinned into his drink. "Shelley and Byron? They were Keats together . . ." (I saw he was ready to sit there and sip his scotch all night.) "Yes," he went on, "we are living history and not just reading it. No cheap concerts or prodigious despairs for me. The Labour Party beggars, in power or out, are worse Imperialists than Kipling. I tell you, the stately homes of England are something we should all regret the passing of; but it's history on the wing and we, you and I, Old Hoss, are here to record it on film—if you'll only travel for us."

"Let's order," I said. "This is one of the few places in the world to prepare haunch of venison California."

"Why California?"

"Because the deer is in season. But later the venison in California is killed by a peculiar local method."

"How, Old Hoss?"

"By automobile."

A TRAVEL PLAN

He ordered another scotch and went back to the attack. "You leave from Boston. There is a plane seat reserved for you there. You fly to Newfoundland and take Imperial Airways to Ireland. By the way, your novels are all on the Index there. They bring a pound each on the book black market in Dublin. You and Shaw and Joyce are the three most popular banned writers there. From Ireland you fly direct to France.

Air France has better planes than usual, but better take up praying again. Then you go to St. Moritz to film the big season."

"What's it all for?"

"A musical film we're planning—going to out-shout Hollywood."

"Got a story line?"

"You can help us get that when you come back with the stock shots. We'll cut in what we need. You can do it. Look, frankly, you have the know-how, as *Fortune* magazine says. You've done this sort of thing better than anyone out here."

Suddenly it seemed a good idea. I could use a change. I had been working a long time in the studios. I had written *The Jolson Story* and done the dialogue for Cecil B. De Mille's *Greatest Show on Earth,* and it was time I got away.

I tried a feeble last excuse. "This will cost a lot of money."

Turtle nodded. "Not a lot, just enough. Shake. We'll have a camera crew and stuff ready for you. Don't worry. It will be a lark."

IF YOU MUST TRAVEL

I went home to pack. Now, traveling is not an art—it's a science and most travelers move out loaded as if they were going to a desert island for their full and natural lives. The less carried the better. My own iron rations for travel I have found the best. Two good suits, one to wear, one in reserve. A really good raincoat and a hat that can be folded into any pocket. Heavy shoes that are comfortable and the needed socks and shirts and underwear, but not too much. Learn to do your dainty things yourself each night. Get your medical shots for the plagues and the ills of the world. And remember, if you're sanitary-minded, the old writer's advice to the young poet about to travel: "Keep your bowels open and your fly closed."

Carry everything in two well-made suitcases and don't bother with a trunk. Carry aspirin, penicillin, and pain-killing pills, and your Vitamin B complexes to round out the world's food values. Also some concentrated canned food

TRAVEL WITH TWO BAGS

for those times you are stranded and they offer you local delights like sheep's eyeballs or snake tripe. Smoke a pipe if you must smoke; cigarettes are hard to come by unless you can afford to smoke pure gold. Pipe tobacco is almost always at hand. Don't bother with cameras unless you're an expert. I'm not and always take people without heads, a rare type. There are plenty of photographs, good ones, to be bought.

Pack enough razor blades, sun glasses, strong scent (bathing and hot water are "an American mistake," you will be told), and simple salves for cuts, germs, and sores of travel.

Several warm sweaters and woolen shirts, a pair of shorts and bathing suit, but you can skip the sun helmet and golf sticks, and learn to cut your own hair. What you can't stuff into two suitcases, leave behind. The less you can do with, the better. But not money. You'll need lots of it. Travel, no matter in what way, costs a lot these days, and no citizen of any port of call goes to bed happy if he hasn't taken the skin

THE ARAB HAS NO PAPER

of an American he's come in contact with that day. Brotherly love and the United Nations do not protect you. An American is fair prey, the fat to be on the natives' unborn children, something sent by Allah or St. Peter to flay and exploit. You will find the good Christians, those that pray the most, the very ones who will strip you the barest. So expect it and travel. Don't get angry or they'll tell you "to go back where you came from."

Carry letters of introduction; they will not do you much

good, but they will impress your purser and your guide. Most people they are addressed to will be out of town or "just leaving." If intimate details offend you, skip the next line. Carry lots of bedbug powder and toilet paper, for most nations raise bedbugs the way we pamper race horses, according to breed and blood lines; and the idea the Chinese and Arabs invented paper is nonsense, for they always reserve some of their digits to replace its need.

2   did God mean us to fly?

I LEFT one dawn after packing one bag and one kit of drawing and painting materials and sharpening a dozen pencils. America looked lush and green and happy as we flew over it. Boston was calm and brown, and the sailboats were moving in ahead of a fast wind. The local airport was long and empty of life as we took off, with a cold wind blowing up our tail feathers. Newfoundland looked just like all dismal pictures of it. It was dank and wet, and the sticky fog lifted only twenty minutes before we took off. Everyone seemed unhappy, and there was a great deal of baggage that looked

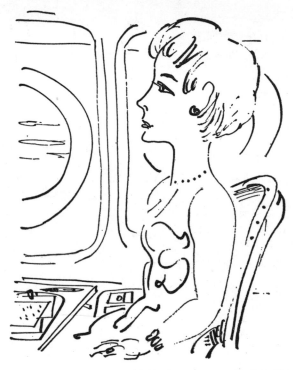

MISS MOLE—FASHION WRITER

like food parcels all around us. I hated the pilot's leer. Egotism is pretty dreadful, in other people.

MISS MOLE AND MISS TONE

A small, pert girl with very red hair and very blue eyes and very good legs sat across the way from me. With her was a tall, lean girl with a good, heroic face and the kind of mouth old waiters fear. She chewed gum and wore two intricate cameras around her shoulders, and looked as if she had seen everything and didn't approve of it. The red-haired one smiled at me and said, "First trip?"

"First this year," I said, making the standard reply to

show I hadn't spent all my life as a member of the Book-of-the-Month Club.

"I'm Miss Mole. This is Miss Tone. My cameraman."

We exchanged details. Miss Tone had hands like a baseball player, and she shook my fingers as if she wanted to be sure I carried no concealed weapons. We were victims of the mutual disaster called travel intimacy, but we no longer fought it.

Miss Mole said, "We're taking some American fashions to Europe to photograph them against European backgrounds. It's a sort of counterinvasion. A protest against European styles taking over American."

"Bulldust," said Miss Tone, closing her eyes and chewing her gum. She was not the talking type unless she could say something destructive. I found out she collected hotel towels, European inn spoons, and even lampshades as proof of her travels.

"Who's sponsoring this invasion?" I asked.

"The American designers and *Fashionable* magazine," said Miss Mole. (*Fashionable* isn't really the name of the magazine, but you get the idea of what kind of publication it is. All the models in it are at least twelve feet high and have green skins. They never smile, seem to suffer from secret diseases, but are dainty and high class, and all look as if the world smelled bad.) *Fashionable* is the kind of magazine that has two hundred pages of ads, and ten pages of text. ("And nothing is ever really *chic*," Miss Tone told me, "unless it's printed in French underworld slang.")

"We are going to show the world," said Miss Mole, "that American fashions are as good as anything they can turn out."

" 'Give me a home where the buffaloes roam,' " sang Miss Tone with closed eyes, after failing to tear out the built-in ashtray. She was bored with the whole idea. She liked to photograph smoking factory chimneys and Death Valley.

"It's an interesting idea," I said. "Ever been abroad before, Miss Mole?"

"No, but the Paris office of *Fashionable* is taking care of everything. There will be professional models at St. Moritz, and we have rooms at the Palace Hotel. Any roaches there?"

Miss Tone groaned. "A fine hotel. They may fly them in air mail."

"Really?" Miss Mole asked.

" 'Bury me not on the lone prair*eee*,' " sang Miss Tone, unsnapping her cameras and getting into a position for sleep. As she dropped off I could just hear the words, " 'and my saddle all covered with *blood*!!!' "

The plane went on with that easy, sliding, seasick slide, half lope, half hiss, that planes have, and at dawn we were in Ireland.

Miss Mole said, "Gee . . . I certainly expected it to be greener—shamrock colored."

THE NEW LOOK IN EUROPE

And after warm milk and small rolls and too much brogue we were off for Paris. Miss Tone had failed to swipe a cobblestone used by St. Patrick. Europe looked about as usual from the air. Once in a while a ruin, once in a great while a rusting tanker or a burned-out ship on the shore. But mostly Europe hadn't changed under those parts we glided over. I felt sad anyway—not that I could find a reason for my gloom.

Paris was interesting from the airport; it smelled the same. That odor of old chestnut leaves, unswept gutters, chicken houses, old wood, and wet newspapers.

Miss Mole said, "It doesn't look so *chic*."

Then we were off again and below the land spread out like

a too-careful toy model, and when the motors lowered their pitch for the landing I woke up and snapped my spine back in place. ("I wish I could carry a spare spine," Miss Tone said, "one to use, and one to travel with.")

Miss Mole was collecting their many bags, and Miss Tone was cursing softly to herself the loss of one of those small light meters that all cameramen carry on strings to impress the rest of us. A fellow collector of travel objects had double-crossed her and snagged it.

"Switzerland," said Miss Mole, "I like it."

"I can almost smell the damn milk chocolate and see the roadside signs," said Miss Tone, who suspected the printed word. . . . She was one of those tall women, beautiful in some mannish manner, with freckles on a pale blue skin that tans like old leather in the sun. She had a smell about her like an old English hunting moor and hounddog puppies. They could have bottled her and sold her as a scent called "Heather and Kennels." She told me she never read a book.

FACTS ON MISS TONE

As I was to get to know her very well, and as she appears in this book a few times, I must explain that no one ever called her anything but Miss Tone. Her first name, she explained, was Mississippi. "Mississippi Tone. How do you like that handle?" And people, when she was a child, shortened the Mississippi to Miss. But she didn't like to be called just Miss. "Hell, that's what they call cigarette girls in night clubs." So she liked to be called Miss Tone. Her friends got used to it. "The rest don't matter."

She had been married several times—the number changed every time she spoke of it, but she was a romantic and looking for male perfection, and not finding it, of course. Miss Tone wasn't a type, but there were a lot of girls like her in the arts,

writing advertising copy, running a business, or raising cattle.
Alert, with sense and wit, and somehow there was no Joe for
them that was the good Joe, the right Joe.

"It's the little cuddly dames that knock off the right husbands. With a wriggle of their little hips and batting their
eyelashes together a few times and looking weak and helpless.
Well, I can't look weak and helpless and so it's no go. I scare
them right Joes away."

"You like traveling?"

"It's all right. I get paid for it."

"You enjoy taking pictures?"

"It's my job. I take good pictures."

"I never could hold a camera."

"Most g.d. writers can't."

Miss Tone said she didn't mind writers; she didn't "think
about them one way or the other." Some people read books so
there must be a buck in the stuff. And she told about a few
writers she knew. She always said "goddamn writers," never
writers.

INSIDE ST. MORITZ

The plane dipped, and far below a cup of vanilla ice cream
took on features, and a frozen lake smiled up at us. Steep
roofs signaled us, and soon we were coming down on a cleared
airfield and many little men with straps around their shoulders were approaching us to take our baggage. It was comfortable—like living in an icebox.

An Alp, close up, is a fearful sight unless it's covered with
snow. It had snowed the night before in St. Moritz. It had
snowed a lot. Very fashionable people, looking like martyrs
or careless fatalists (the type who wear their coats like capes
and never use the sleeves), were passing behind a smoking
horse, their skis making that small birdlike sound that all-

waxed wood makes on packed dry snow. There was a one-lunged hotel bus rattling tire chains, a bored Hungarian ghost, and a man was tearing open Miss Mole's packages and swearing in German, French, and Italian (there being no Swiss language, as any schoolboy knows). Miss Tone, most likely uneducated, not knowing this fact, was trying to appease the customs officer by sign language and a gesture that could only mean: get-away-before-I-knock-your-g.-d.-head-off!

"Trouble?" I asked.

The customs officer snapped the ends of his mustache in rage. "They do not declare anything. They prepare no form. *Il faut vivre, combattre, et finir avec les siens!*"

"What's he saying?"

AT THE CUSTOMS OFFICE

"They only come here to take pictures of the beautiful Swiss landscape, and in front of it they want to pose these clothes."

"But where is the form declaring these garments? *Bitte?*"

"Yes," I said to Miss Mole, "the form. Did your Paris office declare these garments?"

"They said they would wire ahead to a man called Zelkalb who is their man here. He can take care of anything, the Paris office said."

"You hear," I said to the customs man. "Zelkalb."

"Zelkalb is no longer here. He has been caught crossing a border and is in a Displaced Persons camp."

"Zelkalb," I said cheerfully to Miss Mole, "is a D.P. Better wire the Paris office to get another boy and leave the garments here with the customs officer."

"I don't like them called garments. They're Fashions. Styles. Creations."

"Better leave them here and give the man five dollars."

Miss Tone snorted, "I'll give him a bat in the eye."

Miss Mole shook her red hair. "He'd place too much of a value on the eye. Give him the five dollars."

Miss Tone, who seemed to be protecting their money, dived down into her clothing and came up from some secret corner with a bill, and the customs officer tipped his cap and called a cab, the hotel bus having left, and he pinched Miss Mole on the behind (an old European custom). *"En avant, soldats chrétiens."*

"Well, that's one way to make a pass."

ICE AND FASHION

St. Moritz, I saw from the window of the rattling Fiat that served as a cab, had escaped the war. It was another world— another century. Everything looked just as it had before the war, even the people. Of course they looked older. Their faces had taken on wrinkles and their figures weight, and they had lost their hair or gained beards. They didn't seem to remember any past—unless you got them drunk, I found out.

The dinner in the hotel was very fine. Miss Mole and Miss Tone invited me to their table. Miss Tone wasn't happy. She felt the mountains were just as good in Montana, where I gather she had been spawned one cold season between round-up time. Her mother had been a schoolteacher who read Zane Grey, and her father was a man who hated the West even if it had made him very rich. Miss Tone was the tomboy type, and instead of settling down to raise cowhands with the nearest lonely male, she had become a very good photographer. Her only weakness was for beer, silk underwear (hearsay, I admit), and cowboy ballads of which she had the most maddening collection in the world, but no voice.

Miss Mole and I made a fine dinner of partridge cutlets St. Moritz.

A fat blond boy looking very young came over and said, "I'm Fisher, your cameraman. Turtle wired me to meet you here."

"Good. What do we take?" I asked.

"Anything you want," said Fisher, smiling at Miss Mole.

"But what's the story line of the movie?"

"Isn't any. You take any colorful shots you want. Then we run them at the studio and fit a story around them . . . ouch!"

Miss Tone had stepped on his toe. I said, "Is there going to be a musical around these shots?"

Fisher nodded. "It's going to be about a trip around the world, but they'll wait to see what we can film before they get a detailed story line."

"Sounds crazy to me," said Miss Mole.

"That's the picture business," said Fisher. He looked about

nineteen but was really twenty-six, I found out, and had been in the film industry for six months; before that he photographed sewers and made documentary films for the Labour Party. He was very bright, a very good cameraman, and had a great contempt for Hollywood, me, all Americans, Miss Tone, *and* modern art. He was well educated, bigoted, witty, and rather an amazing person, but after a while depressing. Later I found out a lot of young Englishmen were like that, and I wondered what Kipling would have thought of them.

He was not the kind of Englishman they export. We in the United States usually see the English actors playing always in character, or the consuls carrying a bit of Eton's playing field under their fingernails, or businessmen trying to impress us they have no side or swank and who weep over news about illness in the Royal Family. Fisher disliked the Royal Family and told us a lot of scandal about them, most of it untrue, I hope. We sent him on his way and finished our dinner.

MEET ALICE MOLE

Miss Mole let me gab her into a Chablis which made her very talky. She told me she had been married once to a very fine boy who was a Madison Avenue interior decorator who made her very unhappy. That was before she met Miss Tone at a fashion show and, discovering that Miss Tone couldn't spell, Miss Mole was hired to write her fashion captions for her. Something about the way their captions and photographs matched made them a popular team in the fashion world. Miss Mole was sure that some day another man would come into her life. She hoped he would be a second baseman, or a gas-station attendant, or a man who had something to do with trucks. For some reason, Miss Tone said, "Alice (Miss Mole) has a romantic idea of the life truck drivers lead." Miss Tone took a butter knife back to her room as a travel token.

After dinner a wire came from the Paris office of *Fashionable*. Alice took it down to the customs officer, and he passed her packages and she gave him a good cigar and a smile which he misunderstood ("I'll be black and blue"). . . . When she got back to the hotel she showed me all the Fashions. Styles. Creations. Miss Tone was in the bathtub trying to bring life back into her big toes because she had badly frozen them.

" 'I dreamed I saw Joe Hill last night,' " Miss Tone sang in the bathroom. " 'You're dead, you're dead, I said . . .' "

"When is the show?" I asked Alice.

"Tomorrow at noon. I have to mail the stuff back to New York in two days to meet the closing deadline. You all right, honey?"

MISS TONE CARRIES ON

" 'I never died, I never died, said Joe,' " sang Miss Tone from the bathroom. " 'I am alive, I am alive, wherever men can organize.' "

"I mean your toes."

"They'll live," said Miss Tone.

I excused myself and wished them the best as I had to look over the town and get Fisher's camera working.

It was hard to believe up there that Europe was in a bad way, shouting, talking, rearming.

For some odd reason the mailman rides a bicycle on the snowy street. He knows most of the princes, international ladies, exiled royalty, by name. Americans, helping Europe by spending money, were every place. Fisher exposed a lot of color film.

3   the best people

FOR a small town parked away in the southeast of a small country, St. Moritz is very well known—mostly by people who have never been able to afford the trip. Its Alpine slopes are as famous as its martinis (the best bars are out of doors and there is danger of falling snow spoiling your cocktail).

What the lower-class magazines call its "Sybaritic elegance" has survived currency restrictions, postwar misery, and the fall of empires. "Europe needs one such place, just as every flivver needs a gas station," Miss Tone said.

I stayed at the Palace Hotel—their towels are softer—but I heard the Kulm and Suvretta House well spoken of by some of the most charming, endowed loafers in Europe.

The view at St. Moritz is fine from almost any angle, and on a clear day you can see the Italian frontier right down Engadine Valley; few people bother to look. Everyone wants a few weeks of rest and good food before going back home.

I took Alice into Hanselmann's for some of the famous pastries. Four o'clock is, of course, the proper time to eat them but Alice said she could do away with half a dozen at almost any hour.

Alice was a little wee off in her French, I discovered, but

AT THE PALACE HOTEL

she did brave the Italian waiter and order *salade coeur de laitue Reine Claudine* (because it reminded her of a romantic novel), only to discover it was lettuce salad.

She perked up when I took her to the Chesa Veglia for dancing, and a Romanian made improper sounds at her and offered to teach her to samba. He said Europe was in dreadful shape. He had only three days left in St. Moritz.

"What else goes on here?" Alice asked me later.

"Ski running by fools with soft bones, skating, curling matches, chess, and high-stake bridge."

"What about the carbonated water bathing?"

"It tickles."

"Is it good for you?"

"Try jumping into two cases of Pepsi-Cola."

"Who are all these people?" We were on the main street rubbing our red noses, looking for Fisher and his camera.

"They have names like Schaumber-Buxhoeneden, Baron Charles de Lippe, John Zervudachi, M. de la Kuerta, Sixte de Nicholas, Marquis O'Assche, Doblhoff-Parme."

"You're making it all up," said Alice.

I went up to two people knocking snow off their overshoes.

"Prince Abdel Corvissiano, Baron Taky-Hesse, meet Miss Mole of *Fashionable* magazine."

"Pleased," said the prince.

"Hi," said the baron, a movie fan.

"Gee," said Alice, when they went on, "what are those badges they are wearing?"

"They are members of the exclusive Corviglia Club. Only a mere ninety people in the whole world can be members."

"Could I see it?"

"How pretty are your models?" I asked.

"Very."

I agreed to see if the club needed a tonic. The club did.

The Corviglia Club is above the village, and a few of the medium-class Dukes of Alba run it. They are hawk-faced, tottering old men who like guests connected with U.S. Steel, General Motors, AT&T, Metro-Goldwyn-Mayer, and owners of Chihuahua dogs; at least I saw no other kind of dogs at the club. There were also two Rothschild barons getting their load of ultraviolet rays at six thousand feet.

The rest of the members, I noticed, preferred *Kirschwasser*, *Cointreau*, Holland gin, and assorted wines, and *pâté de foie gras* on crackers.

The members were impressed by the models, Alice Mole by the members, and Miss Tone by the cloud formations— "The color of *crème de menthe* over the club," she said.

At four we had tea, *madeleines, baba au rhum,* and a lot of drinks Alice now called *apéritifs.*

"La bonne aventure," said a baron, a playwright who stole from the Hungarian, to Alice as the models reviewed a few Fashions, Styles, and Creations.

"American," said Alice with pride.

"Une vieille rengaine. The evils of moderation are never mentioned in polite society."

"All union labor."

"Raide et très audacieuse."

"Made from Southern cotton goods."

"Qui trouvent la mariée trop belle."

"California leather belts," said Alice.

"Tétons de Venus," said the baron, and I led Alice away before her R. H. Macy French caught up with her.

It was a fine afternoon and we only lost one of the models, but as she was on loan from the Paris office of *Fashionable* Miss Tone left a description of her, *une petite mare d'eau,* with directions she be returned when found. A chargé d'affaires promised to take care of it and stood us some *Lieb-fraumilch* and *Pernods,* and we went back to the hotel.

AMERICAN OUTPOSTS

I left the next day for Berlin, and the last thing I saw at the airport was Miss Mole loading her bundles into the westbound plane . . . and Miss Tone singing to the customs officer:

> *"Hang up your coat*
> *And spit on the wall*
> *Choose your partners*
> *And promenade all!"*

The customs officer nodded politely and said, *"Ja. Behüte euch Gott . . ."* and just then a huge bronze ashtray marked "Palace Hotel" dropped out of Miss Tone's sleeve. Alice was so shocked she *almost* dropped the cigarette lighter in the form of one of Michelangelo's "Bound Captives" that used to adorn the hotel clerk's desk.

My plane pulled out just then—Fisher just made it—and I brooded all the way to the German border on the fact that at a certain point we all discover virtue is inconsistent with our vices . . .

There are a lot of American troops in Europe (a top sarge yelling, "Get the lead out, you lugs," just like in the movies). And French troops and some English. They seem to like their job and beef about it and drink the local wine and beer and escort the girls around and get in trouble about it, I was told, just like soldiers all over the world.

An expert could look at them and their American tanks and American guns and tools and give you an idea of coming events. The future of armored divisions, the fighting courage of French soldiers, the ability of the General Staff, and where the next war will be lost or won. Frankly, I couldn't. I just talked to the boys and saw them in the rain and saw them in the sun. Marching, drinking, griping, standing still and whistling at a broad. They seemed young and not too earnest, and certainly had no real idea of what it was all about, and didn't want to know.

There were also men and officers with the shoulder patches of the United Command and the Western Army. But of them, I have even a vaguer impression. Every place there were the Germans, not at all defeated, just whining they hadn't lost the war, had just been betrayed by Hitler (whom they still secretly admire) and they had rights, and they wanted rights, and they were entitled to rights. It's not easy to like a German and I didn't try. They have no guilt complex, they deny the evil, the slaughter of the concentration camps, and if you show them the pictures, they say they were "faked in Hollywood." Their main energy is spent in promoting a war between Russia and the U.S. and they hope we blow both our heads off . . .

BERLIN—POSTWAR STYLE

Berlin—the city once of the best *Deutscher Hof*—is a wonderful sight if you remember all the evil the Germans have done in the world, if you recall the millions of dead, tortured, and starved and burned in furnaces. It's a real wreck from the air, a cracked series of anthills. Closer up on the *Tauentzienstrasse* the fat-necked businessmen and the big blonde mares of women—*Hausfrauen*—are very busy setting up business and taking in as much loot as they can from anyone in sight. They are better fed at the *Stammtisch* than the English and the French, they are happier than the Italians and a great many American taxpayers that I know. The cops, the *Schupos*, look like the storm troopers they are.

Many of the streets are loaded with new, fashionable shops. Cafés and the night life are foul and evil, the black-market boys, the under-the-counter lads, and the whores, fags, and night citizens live high. It's not a nice thing to see the German whining and eating, bellowing his rights, and peddling jewels stolen from murdered Czechs, Jews, Austrians, Danes,

BERLIN STREET

and other people they have mutilated with their *Panzerwagen*. The old Nazis are doing fine.

There are poor people, of course, living in holes and walled-in doorways and in the buildings being repaired. But even the German poor have that stiff neck and that way of saying, "*Wie, bitte?* We didn't want that war, and nothing is true about those concentration camps, the damn Reds and Americans and Jews just invented the whole thing. Our *Lust-knaben* were heroes."

"What about the future?"

They smile slyly. "There will be a war. *Endkampf gegen* whom? The Russians will fight the Americans and both will wipe each other out. And the one that comes out a little better, we Germans will join them and show them how to rule the world for *Gleichschaltung*."

This may sound crude (it does—let's face it). But it's about what you will often hear from lots of Germans if an *Amerikaner*—you—buy them a drink, give them a tip, or let them steal your cigarettes. They don't like the Americans any better than the Russians, but they feel the Americans are soft and sentimental enough not to let the Russians push them around too much. *Macht und Erde*—power and earth are still German gods.

FACING THE IRON CURTAIN

You can see all the Russians you want to at the border zone, as Berlin is deep in the Red part of Germany, but under four-power control. You can visit the Red section, but I didn't. The Red guards looked tough and mean, and all day and night the two radio systems shout at each other and spray the air with remarks and events that no one really pays any attention to as they drink beer and chew *salmis de faisans*.

The German under our control broadcast names of Germans working for the Reds, and the Reds broadcast real news such as: California is being abandoned at once because of lack of water, that revolts of thousands of sharecroppers are breaking out again, that Negroes are fleeing Confederate Army lynch mobs in cities, and that warmongers have infiltrated the Boy Scouts. All in *verdammte Hochdeutsch*.

It made very little sense; there was an odor of evil, some sinister smell of trouble under control. I didn't stay long, as I saw nothing to film, and decided to go on to Paris. Fisher was above it all; he kept cleaning his camera lens and say-

AMERICAN SOLDIER IN EUROPE

ing, "A hell of a lot of good it did to win the bloody effing war. England ought to lose the next one and let America rebuild it, the way you chaps are taking care of the effing Huns and the other *Dummköpfe*."

He had something there, I told him, but it didn't seem practical somehow. Fisher brooded all the way to Paris. His mother and three sisters had been killed by a V-2 in London during the Blitz. His brother had lost an arm at Dunkirk, his uncle had gone mad at Tobruk, and Fisher had an idea he was due soon to be sent to Malaya on active jungle service . . .

Meeting the American soldier in Europe and trying to catch an impression of his thinking is hard. Some know what it's all about, some don't. But in many is the core of standing on earth and fighting back, standing as long as they can and offering whatever they are able to carry to throw at the enemy. It's, some remember, a dirty business done in dreadful places. It's a mean business done bravely and in hot agony under pressure.

INNOCENTS ABROAD AGAIN

The soldier in his moment of dirty power is very human, I found. He is busy at his special trade and he has no neatness of stance, no gesture out of Greek art. The art of the soldier is not to look like art and that's why I saw early that most of all battle painting is false. Goya caught it, Guys, some of the early Grosz, and that is about all. It is only true, one boy told me, "when the soldier is you, when the face is someone close to you, when but for the grace of something, the blot on the ground, the mess under the tank, the puzzle in the doctor's hands might be you."

For the soldier there are no good wars, no needed wars, no bore wars. His war is the most important thing of his life, it's the war he knows, feels, smells, and tastes. Pictures bring away only the ghost of things as they are, the lines and colors of men who have made more history than they can consume.

4   I remember Paris

BACK in Paris, I shipped the film to London with Fisher and sat down to hear from Turtle.

The city had taken on a new mood since my last trip. The Ritz Bar in Paris is the only thing in the world that never seems to change. The same people seem to lean against it as usual, digesting a little alcohol, telling the same stories, and worrying, it appears, about the same girls called Alice, Reba, Helene, and an old-fashioned type (out of the novels of Alphonse Daudet) called either Sappho or Louisa.

A tall, bright-looking girl with yellow hair came up to the bar, and I remembered that ten years ago she had been an American art student with lots of talent but too much money.

"What are you doing here?" she asked.

"Traveling."

"You used to be a newspaperman?"

"Almost anybody can say that, Minnie," I admitted.

"Look, I could use you. I've bought *The Paris Word*."

The Paris Word (that's as good a name as any for it, here) was an old English-language newspaper published in Paris. About every twenty years it changed hands at a great loss to all concerned, but no one seemed to mind that.

I said, "That costs a lot of money."

"I have it. What are you drinking?"

"Martinis with a spiced onion."

"I'll have a drink with oranges in it. Any drink with orange

MINNIE DRANK ORANGE JUICE

juice," said Minnie. "Well, how about it? I have the backing."

I remembered that Minnie had married a Californian
named, let's say, Bartlett, whose grandfather had stolen half
the state by getting a contract to build a railroad, and Washington would pay him a million dollars a mile for rails laid
on level ground and six million dollars a mile for rails
laid across the Rocky Mountains. By moving the Rocky Mountains west sixty miles (on his map), Bartlett's grandfather
had become a railroad king.

"Why an English-speaking newspaper in Europe?"

"It's a great tradition," Minnie said, sipping gin and
orange bitters.

"An expensive one."

She made the stock answer of all rich Americans in Europe.
"It's deductible."

She told me a lot of secrets about postwar Europe—none
of them of much use in a book, because in a week they have
no value. I had a few more and went back to my hotel.

THE POSTMAN DOESN'T RING AT ALL

I expected a letter from the U.S. and I got up early
and sat in the small lobby. The yellow stuff on the window
panes turned out to be sunlight. The postman came, and I
remembered him from my art-school days. I offered him
some wine and he sat down and said thanks and a lot more.

"How is it here?" I asked.

"We begin by capitulation," he said. "Now the Americans
are coming back. I admit it. Every place from the Tuileries
to the Latin Quarter there are Americans asking for rooms,
and you know it's like before the war, only, well . . . we,
we aren't like before the war, and the Americans who are
asking for the rooms aren't like before the war either, but
what is, is, I keep telling everyone. We used to laugh on both

THE MAILMAN

sides of the face, remember? Now, we worry and feel pain and get very tender, and it's like—well, even a postman feels it in the weight of his letters. We've experienced something like annihilation and this rebirth is cold and so tragic—only those with some mania or genius feel fully alive in it."

"You're a smart man," I said.

"We struggle," the postman said, "and grunt so with a dilemma, a dilemma of grace under pressure, you understand . . . a dilemma of human dignity (if you don't laugh at those words), of birth, love, tenderness, passion—and we never solve any of the dilemma. But we make poses, as you Americans say, we strike attitudes."

He had been a law student and a schoolteacher, he told
me, but carrying mail was all he felt comfortable doing.

I said, "The intellectual has his problems."

"But we go on. That's the main thing, I say—you have to
go on. Try stopping and even the stones seem to rot. I respect survival. I tip my hat to it."

"Sure," I said. "I feel that way, too."

"Everything here isn't dead or changed. You understand
it isn't like the old days when everybody had it and used it,
or spent it, or hoarded it."

"I know."

"It's been very cold and there isn't any coal really, and
not much wood and this coat is my army jacket dyed, and
if you go down to the fringe of the city, you can see the real
hunger in people's faces and the pale yellow skin, unwashed
most likely, and you smell the sourness, the real postwar
smell."

"That's an unpopular look at Paris—like at a war."

THE INTELLECTUAL'S VOICE

"But let's not talk about wars (he had another drink).
There is poverty, there is politics—always politics—enough
to go around for everybody. We French produce more than
we can consume, I always say. But there are still the girls:
fat ones, thin ones. They are the same, like before the war
—no?"

"No—maybe because I'm older."

"Yes, perhaps you'll find it isn't the same as it used to
be, and perhaps it's better for us to be hungry and cold and
work a little harder (if such things are virtues)—it's certainly a changed world."

"In some ways . . . some ways not."

"Oh, there are still the rich, with the fat red glands on
their necks, and they suck up the best of everything and

really their world isn't changed. Not much from what it was
—only you know—if you watch them closely when you hand
them some flat, thin, dirty letter—even the stamps are patched
sometimes—their faces turn the color of dirty paper and they
open their lips like fish and pant, and they seem to be ready
to be sick in your mailbag."

"It's worse in England, I hear."

"What I started to say was that the Americans are coming
back and that's a good sign, and maybe soon they'll whistle
again *L'amour est enfant de Bohème* and brag about flush
toilets."

"You and I were here then," I said.

"I can't say it's such a bad thing to be alive even if there
is no coal and the children have yellow faces."

"What do you think of the future?"

"Do you read much? But of course you were always getting books by the post. Once in a while now I like to take
down *Mémoirs d'Outre-tombe*. It's very old and tattered—
my wife, she sold the bindings, you understand, during the
war—they make cigarette trays out of the old leather—but
the pages—most of them are still there. I remember on cold
nights reading, 'France is the heart of Europe . . . one can
judge the distance from it . . . by the degrees of animation
or languor of the country into which one retires . . .' "

"I like that," I said.

"Perhaps this isn't really true, you understand, we're so
cynical at times we get very sentimental to make up for it.
Everyone says such things of us. *Ce sont des histoires
amusantes . . .*"

"Paris—you love it," I said.

"Well," he got up to go, "you'll see us now like men shot
to the moon by rocket and looking longingly back on earth,
only nothing ever really focuses the way it used to, does it?"

"No—we're getting old."

LET'S NOT TALK ABOUT WARS

"*Nous avons étudié nos leçons.* Thank you for the wine. If any of those letters come, *United States of America,* with the crinkly green paper inside, I'll send my daughter over with it fast. Well, anyway, it's good to see the Americans again, out of uniform . . ."

"Don't get flat feet," I said.

A LETTER FROM SWEDEN

After the postman left, I sat down and wrote out our talk. It was so different from what the unidentified taxi driver or charwoman is supposed to have said in *Time.*

Then I opened my mail. There was an interesting letter from a friend traveling in Sweden.

> . . . It saddens and embarrasses me [the letter said] that the bottle of *Brännvin* is not bigger. Visitors to Sweden are issued food-ration coupons and (if they request it) a liquor allowance on the basis of the intended time of sojourn. And the amount of hard likkah which I was assumed to consume during my short stay there was one-half liter. So you *get* one-half liter. I dispatched it to you today by prepaid express.
>
> If you are not intimately conversant with these Swedish beverages, perhaps you will not construe it as an act of paternalism if I venture a fragment of commentary as to the use of this fluid. *Brännvin* (which means "burnt wine") or *Akvavit*, its other name, is not to be poured at room temperature and sipped like sherry—though many Americans do it, I see in the bars. In Sweden it is chilled and served with that heavily spiced raw herring which they have over there. The diner impales a piece of herring on his fork, pops it into his mouth, swallows it with a minimum of mastication, and then downs a small jigger of *Brännvin* at one gulp. No sipping.
>
> It is this constant and repetitive consumption of raw spiced herring and *Brännvin* (or *"snaps"*) which has made Sweden such a happy hunting ground for dat ole debbil ulcer. By the time a man is your age and mine, he has usually got a fine assortment of ulcers; and a woman in Stockholm giving a dinner party is fully prepared to have two or three of the prospective guests ring her on the morning of the even and say that she regrets they won't be able to come tonight because Gustav's ulcers are kicking up again. (Not that you are in any danger of snagging an ulcer on half a liter of the stuff!)
>
> In Sweden *Brännvin* is not just *Brännvin* and that's that. There are more than a score of different kinds. Basi-

SPICED HERRING AND BRANNVIN

cally all are merely alcohol, sometimes made from potatoes, sometimes from trees. The difference is that the
various kinds are laced with different spices to produce
the different names. In color, the various kinds range
from *Brännvin* which is as clear as spring water through
all shades of pale yellow and saffron to a fairly rich yellow. And anybody who makes any pretense of knowing
what is what will have his own brand which he prefers
and which he orders by name when in a public restaurant. At a relatively simple home dinner, the guest would
be served the choice of the house—whichever his host
prefers. But at a more formal dinner the guests are often
given a choice of two or even three different kinds of

Akvavit . . . Even I, a ruddy foreigner, have a favorite kind.

I don't know how extensive your preoccupation may be in the arcana of alcohol, but it might mildly amuse you to take a quick gander at a copy of the Swedish Liquor Monopoly's catalogue, which I enclose . . . *"Helbut"* is an abbreviation for *"Helbutelj"* meaning a whole bottle, usually approximately a quart. *"Halvbut"* means a half-bottle or about a pint. The figures under *"Helbut"* and *"Halvbut"* are in Swedish crowns and you can flop any of them into rough dollar equivalents by dividing by five—except that in many instances on these sheets the prices are no longer valid. Most of them have been doubled, in accord with the avowed policy of the greatly overestimated Social Democratic party of Sweden to make life as drear and drab as possible for the poor, harassed citizenry.

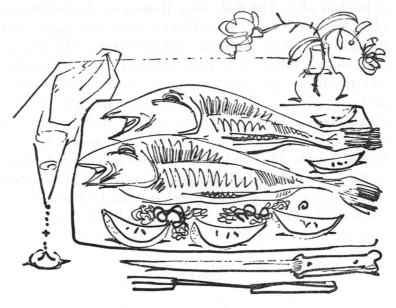

LUNCH

5   tourists and natives

THE rest of Paris is just about what the tourist sees: sole *Joinville,* duck *Perigueux,* fair hotels, *Grises Gitanes* cigarettes, and the Banque de France, Lazare Frères, and characters *un peu exaltés,* and what you find on the black market, what you see in the streets. So much has been written about it that there is no use repeating what you read in every travel book. But under it all I had a sense of something wrong and I wish I were wise enough to discover what it was. *Toujours joyeux* is just talk.

The French are ruled by a system so baffling to an American that it looks, on the surface, like mere corruption of office. Everyone grafts, everyone sells his vote to what he thinks is the best offer. The Reds offer Heaven on the installment plan. De Gaulle offers it in Hitler's made-over pants. And the Church, and Big Business, and the Manure Mob (farmers), and the Village Boys (wine-makers), and the Shipping and the Military (despots from North Africa or Indo-China) all have a party, and all elect like mad and talk a lot. And in the end France manages to just keep going. Walter Lippmann may see it differently, but only in other words, because France is not healthy. And politics has become a racket as bad as the worst we have had. Bernard Shaw once told me in an interview that "man is not a political animal," but he never did know the French. They are mostly political animals and certainly prove what others have said: that with the French,

CITIZEN OF PARIS

democracy is not ever a fact, only a tradition, as they politely
hiss *"Merci bien."*

Meanwhile they amuse themselves, eat well, at least a lot
of them do. They are very decorative, have the proper ideas
about passion (and often love), continue to be the art capital
of the world (only all their great modern masters are dying
off and nothing new is being done). Emotionally I understand them, feel and taste them, but politically, economically,
it really doesn't make much sense. The kilometers run on to
Reims, St. Quentin, Guise, as usual, but France is sick. What
makes sense is their fear of the rearming of Germany. There,
I hear, they are true to facts and the only realists in Europe.
I met a lawyer I knew, a real French lawyer—a *maître de
requêtes*—right out of Daumier, and we had a few coffees
and he explained it to me clearer than anyone has before.

THE GREAT FEAR

"You see, we know the Germans. They are savage, the
kind Caesar found in Gaul, their asses painted blue and their
heads rimmed in bronze. Dressed in furs, breeding their
blonde cows of women, they grew big and they haven't
changed. They are perfect in certain things. They keep very
clean like a good cat. They follow orders like a trained ape,
and they fight well, like a bulldog trained to hang on to a
rabbit's throat till it dies."

"You don't like them," I said ironically.

"No, I don't. I don't trust them. They're not just mad
actors out of Wagner's crazy operas. Their Bible *is* the Ring
operas, and Hitler's slogans. They still believe them all,
you know. I've just come from Frankfort and all the old
Nazis are back in power, thanks to the United States. *Tant
pis pour vous."*

"I know that's a mistake, but the Military do things like that."

"Now we're arming them again. And someplace a secret general staff is meeting and planning another war, and aimed at France . . . Three times they have invaded us. It's a habit . . . Why not again?"

"Will they fight the Russians? That's all that interests Americans."

"No! They'll join the Russians first chance they get. Then they'll wait for the Russians to make a mistake, and they'll own Europe yet. Maybe the world."

"This talk is depressing," I said.

We agreed on that, and had lunch. Back at the hotel there was a wire to come to London. Turtle liked the film shots and wanted to try and work out a story line for the rest of the picture.

I was to come to London. But first I had a date to take Miss Tone out to dinner. Alice was busy covering fashion shows.

ON THE TOWN

The ale at the English café on Montparnasse is served in big china mugs and the little green onions are free. The tables are in the back room under dusty pictures of McKinley's funeral, the burial of Queen Victoria, and a framed picture of Franklin Roosevelt's body being escorted in state to Hyde Park. It gave one the evasive nuances of one's own past, an old tinny player piano ground out "Diga Diga Do."

There was an old-fashioned tall stove in the center of the room, and three cats, all called Henri, slept on the sawdust of the worn floor. We ordered boiled beef and horse-radish sauce. I ordered two fresh mugs of ale. Someone had carved into the tabletop: *Le mal de mer n'existe pas* . . .

'I'm sorry I was busy this afternoon," I said.

"Skip it, chum."

Miss Tone pushed back her plate and took out fixings and rolled herself a cigarette.

The waiter set a plate of boiled beef before us; his big red nose made a perfect isosceles triangle.

"Pass me the horse-radish, Stevie. Nothing is perfect in this world, only boiled beef. How do you feel about love?"

"I'm polite to it."

"Good for you. I'm in a bad way."

"Going into it?" I asked.

"Coming away from it."

"You're lucky."

"So is a slaughterhouse hog."

"Maybe."

We had a lot more ale in sedate radiance, horse-radish sauce needs a lot of ale. It was a very pleasant, good evening, appetizing and delectable. We went to a dive in the Eighteenth Arrondissement and drank more ale, then we went down to the market and had them broil us some lobsters and Miss Tone wanted to try the market beer, and by that time it was early in the morning and we couldn't find a cab in the fetid light, but we did pick up and lose a *vendeuse* from the Galeries Lafayette.

I think it was later, but it may have been before, that Miss Tone had a fight with a hotel doorman. But I am sure where I bought her the Spanish scarf. A little place with candlelight, and a fat girl who oiled her skin with something for *l'atmosphère,* who told us our fortunes. Miss Tone was very happy with the brand of brandy they had here. And *les digestifs* and *demies.* She told me the story of her life.

I remember sitting in Miss Tone's hotel room and she sang *"un bel dì vedremo"* from *Madame Butterfly* until she grew tired.

She suddenly looked at her hands, contrite and humble and sad, and then whistled in a puzzled way, or rather tried to whistle, and then she turned toward me and fell flat on her face, like a tree falling, fantastically steady and solid. She lay with elegance and serenity. I got her to bed and turned out the lights and as I reached the door I heard her say, "Why do we cut across the biological grain? Love moved in and couldn't close the door . . ."

"Goodnight, Miss Tone, go to sleep," I said.

There was a snore from the bed like a half-asphyxiated dog, as if the tired brain had given up groping for a phenomenon beyond it.

I went out, and feeling like the interior of a rotten walnut, I walked slowly to my hotel.

The next day it rained and was foggy. I could not fly to London, I would have to take the channel train.

I called Miss Tone. "Baby," she said, "Tone is hung over as a mountain goat's rear end. But thank you for the use of your company."

THE CHANNEL TRAIN

"Non other lyfe is worth a bene; for wedlock so easy and so clene," I read in my pocket copy of Chaucer.

The great echoing train station was a busy place, the smoking gold fog bouncing off the ochre roof, and the grind of diesels under the very floor that I sat on shaking the walls. Walls the color of melancholy sherry, the color of the enameled avaricious nose of the ticket seller. The setting was perfect.

Sitting under the monstrous deformations of advertising posters I waited for my train. People passed with a pumping motion of the knees, earnestly unhappy, as if defrauded of their dreams. The children yawned and wailed.

Too bad all planes were grounded by fog. Still, I didn't mind, thinking of the soggy Channel crossing, that spear of sea between two nations. At last my train was ready . . .

In the night darkness the train cut across three rivers and still the land slept and the people in it. The click of the wheels kept time with the pulse in my head. Click, click, click. A sharp, painful catechism. An idiot's stutter as the *wagon-lit* went on, the engine giving that pansy whistle. I felt part of things, doing my share in world events to make civilization last just a little longer—even if only by making motion pictures.

How quickly the past had changed, I thought. People are always asking me what kind of people did you know in those days between two world wars, and I can only answer they were just people, even if they wore Molyneux pajamas, played *chemin de fer* and ate *Bel Paese* cheese with *Strega*. Almost all their class did. They could be trusted not to put conversation to improper political use, and if their ideas were thinning out in patches they wore their personalities gaily, like a gypsy's rags. They shot things, in Africa, but no longer thought everything decadent was Persian poetry. I don't think they felt very different from other people, but they worked too hard at being different.

They gave money *pour les pauvres de M. le Curé*, they bred staid elderly spaniels who were doped on the white meat of chicken, and some had disembodied, abstracted qualities that showed they were worried at the way the world was going, but were too polite to speak up. It was hard to dislike them, it was easy to be sorry for them.

They had, I admit, the sadness of a goal achieved—complete boredom. They were like long-defunct music trapped in old halls. A countess from Kansas used to say, "Poor dears, they were once the salt of the earth and the earth was being

WELL-HEELED PEOPLE

attacked by a terrible epidemic of hatred." I liked her for saying that; she also wasn't a snob, just bored.

THE JUST-GONE PAST

There were all kinds in Europe in those days. They had their lunatic fringe that lived their own way of life while the world went up in flames, but even they, I sometimes felt, were so conditioned that they could not change without admitting a sad truth: the present is never what it should be. They had no time to think of the future, or perhaps they couldn't think, really know.

"Life is an onion," the wittier ones said, "no wonder we

weep as we devour it . . ." (This may not sound amusing now, but it seemed amusing then.) At least it was all easy to listen to.

Some of them died of vice or drink or fashionable doctors, and they erected them monuments that pleased no one but their dogs. Others gave up and said, "Marriage often leads to love," and some said, "Everything soon becomes yesterday," and we laughed, for a rich man's joke is always funny. The times appeared less serious then or they acted as if they were.

As the era drew to a close and World War II came near, and the shape of the world changed from round to flat, about the only thing that didn't change among the rich Americans in Europe was the habit of eating. Even people who were no longer hungry and who watched the storm warnings with one eye still felt they owed it to themselves to have the truffles and Molossol caviar, the tasty Czechoslovakian pâté . . . and of course, the orange Earl Grey tea. It was no use talking to them about the end of the world when they could still own a few dozen *terrines* of pâté de foie gras, and a cellar full of *Roederer*. Of course we prowlers into their society, we too, helped them eat up their surplus. We didn't feel shy either about it. We were always hungry. . . .

The train ran on and I remembered it was easy to face a world breaking up with an omelet with artichoke hearts, lobster *ravigote*, pilaf of sweetbreads and stuffed olives. They might be shivering on street corners in Warsaw, polishing tanks in Berlin, but a brine-soaked *risotto* of mussels and lobster and lamb and chicken sleeping with ease on a bed of saffron rice was no help to the Munich crisis. When the writers and artists became worried, they always cured themselves by asking, what did they own: nothing!

"*Heiliger Gott im Himmel!*" a Chicago Republican in Dresden used to shout when he counted his holdings. "A man can't live on the dividends of U.S. Steel! Those Wall Street *Schweinehund, Sauhaufen Drecksäcke!*"

It was as if World War II was already begun, and they were digging tank traps around their villas, piling up their mink coats to keep out the seepage of poison gas they were sure was going to be used against the Lido, the Place Vendôme, the Rock at Cap d'Antibes, the Bar Basque at Menton, the Ritz. They were scared, too scared to admit times were changing. They weren't all bad—just half-bad, as I remembered them.

They floated in oceans of turtle soup and sherry, and rode out the rise of Hitler on saddles of venison with *Meinkraut*. They were sad over the *fricadelles* with *sauce piquante*, the calf's head *en tortue*, the *bécasses flambées* . . . and they drank, when they could afford it, *Le Lait du Pape* (a vintage wine), made for the Vatican—toward whom many prayed as toward Mecca, falling to silk-clad knees in hopes that they would have the courage, when the time came, to leap from the Pont Neuf, Pont Royal, Pont Louis XVI (they never thought of the Pont Alexandre III, which was always too crowded to make a good decent death). It was easy to think of them like this; for most of them fled to America and did well by the war.

Yes, there was no doubt about it, "the best people" (of course made up of people who called themselves the best people) were getting a little dull and a little frayed, but between the two world wars there was a new kind of American coming over. Hard-faced men with slit eyes and new evening clothes that had room under the left armpit for a lump of leather and shiny blue steel. They talked Chicago or Brooklyn, and they used such words as hood, hist, chiv, and rub-out. They were all perfectly legal, you understand; their only crime was that their income tax returns were not in order, and "the guy with the whiskers," as they called Uncle

Sam, had put them on the lam. There were a lot of them. I did not find them the charming romantics most people did . . .

LANDSCAPE AT NIGHT

The train hooted for a crossing and I was back in the present—and they were all gone, and their era—and Europe was in a bad way, a newer, grimmer way.

CHANNEL TRAIN

The towns, the cities, flew past and the steel ribbons of rails ran on ahead, waiting for the puffing train. Signal arms waited. Red and green spots pinpricked the night.

The stone houses were bone white in the moonlight. Lamps were few and spread in skimpy patterns in the throbbing darkness. Crops grew and tossed in the night wind, and at crossroads the trucks waited, loaded with life and food and drink for Paris. Mist rimmed many meadows. Early cows

chewed fog. I pressed my head against the glass and wondered if this was the same land of fashion designers, drunks,
greed, fear, smart chat, and international accents I knew in
the daylight. It looked calm and uninterested in such things.
So still and asleep.

The train went on, blowing a ghastly thin whistle at road
crossings. A sharp, spreading sound that went up to roll
against the ghost hills and come re-echoing back to hammer
at my temples with more questions than I cared to answer
. . . The Channel looked cold and rough. Some odd-looking
men ignored me in *too* pointed a manner . . . haters of
Americans . . .

THE ENGLISH CARRY ON

6   Turtle's island

TURTLE was having breakfast in the dingy hotel dining room. He smiled when he saw me.

"Looking very sinister in that hat."

I said, "It's my square head."

"How does England look to you, Stevie?"

"Like an old lady who recovered *too* well from a dangerous operation. What's the matter with all of Europe?"

"I just read something by D. H. Lawrence about false sentiment. Here, let me read it to you:

"Sentimentalism is the working off on yourself of feelings you haven't really got. We all *want* to have certain feelings: feelings of love, of passionate sex, of kindliness, and so forth. Very few people really feel love, or sex passion, or kindliness, or anything else that goes at all deep. So the mass just fake these feelings inside themselves. Faked feelings! The world is all gummy with them. They are better than real feelings, because you can spit them out when you brush your teeth; and then tomorrow you can fake them afresh."

"That's one Europe," I said.

Turtle smiled and closed the book. "All Europe is one Europe. There is *only* one; maybe that is why we're always in such trouble. I used to think it was several Europes until I went to Zurich in 1917 to see about some American film firms that were doing business with the Germans through the Swiss banks . . . an old trick, and I went to a small café to drink *Riesling,* and a short, broad man with a little beard was smoking Jaunes cigarettes at a small table and talking very earnestly to a group of men. He was called Nikolai Lenin (I remember the name of the café now—the Odeon). And sitting by the stove was another small, bearded man with thick glasses, smoking a Voltigeur cigar and drinking Swiss *Neufchâtel,* and he was talking earnestly to a group of young men. Later when I went back often to the café they said he was called James Joyce . . . And every night when I went there, there were the two men with the little beards. . . . Neither, by the way, had ever attracted the attention of any newspaper readers at that time."

"That's your one Europe?" I asked.

"That's everyone's one Europe. Side by side . . . one was going to overthrow the crowned heads, the other smash the limits of the novel. Some place today are sitting two or three men . . . unknown . . . unpublished, hungry, tired, ill,

happy, diseased, healthy, wounded, well fed, lousy . . .
planning to change Europe again."

"I don't expect any Englishmen among them," I said.

"You always expect the English—I mean, the ruling classes
in England—to change for the better and they disappoint
you. The labels change: they say Labour, or Tory, or So-
cialist, or Reactionary, but it's really the same old Empire
keeping a world of white and black niggers in their places
for a neat twenty per cent. Join me at lunch?"

"Yes, any real food left?"

"Maybe."

THE LAST ROAST BEEF OF ENGLAND

LONDON STREET TALK

We went to Hatchett's old restaurant in Piccadilly, and
then, after a proper roast beef and Yorkshire pudding, and
that ale that was as good as it always was in certain places,
we walked around the Serpentine in Hyde Park. Turtle

seemed happy. His ulcers were at rest and he was wrapped warmly in his topcoat and carrying his rolled umbrella.

"I have been reading Santayana again, Stevie. I guess I still have a Low Presbyterian provincial kind of prejudice toward him."

"He's a funny old man—Europe's last laughing writer, now that Shaw is dead," I said.

Turtle rattled his umbrella against a railing. "You forget he himself believes in nothing, really. I remember his lines: 'The Church is too human . . . too good to be true. I simply cannot believe that nature can conform so closely to the heart's desire.' "

"What else did you get out of him, Turtle?"

"I once lived with one of his followers in a boarding house in South Kensington, this was years ago . . . and I could, then anyway, see what he was trying to say, second hand, of course, through this boy."

"What?" I expected something really world-shaking.

Turtle stopped and scratched in the loose, damp earth border of the park path. "Let me say it slowly . . . it adds up to this: Some of us are really hunting for the spiritual possibility of conquering the vanities and engrossments of our personal self in a howling, competitive world . . ."

I shook my head. "A little *too* simple."

"Maybe. Stevie, I'll show you the new London since the war."

It hadn't changed so much since I had been there in '41 during the Blitz, only they had cleaned it up and were trying to rebuild St. George's Hospital across from Hyde Park where I had helped them carry in the wounded; Savile Row, and the little brick dust place near Harrod's where I had bought my neckties; the Tate Gallery had its pictures back (and the Turners were as alive as ever); and there was, as usual, St. Paul's and Old Bailey against the tarnished silver

BACK IN '41

sky. But I no longer heard the ack-ack guns, or the thud of time bombs being exploded in the Hackney Marshes. The Schweppes lime drink wasn't what it had once been, Turtle said, but to me it tasted as usual. And the Lord Chancellor's Court was being repaired; at the Odeon they were again playing Shakespeare. And Turtle and I had some gin and tonic.

Turtle held his stomach—I knew his ulcers were talking to each other. He turned pale and said, "Let's talk about the movie . . . Have you licked the story line yet?"

London—"oranges and lemons say the bells of St. Clement's"—has a charm of its own, and yet it was depressing.

Everyone looked shabby, a lot looked underfed, and the grime on the old buildings was darker and a lot of the bombed-out places were still bare. The English eat worse than anyone in Europe. The French eat better, the Germans eat better and dress better. "England won the war but is still living on war rations," they all say, and there seems no hope in sight. No matter who is in control, the way seems only down under the dome of St. Paul and the steps of the British Museum.

The British are people to be admired, and I have always liked them, except for those times in their Colonial ideas when they push people around and they try to play footsie with the reactionaries all over the world to bolster up their tin or oil or rubber shares. One can forgive them. They are a proud, noble, and very brave people, part of Westminster Bridge, Blackfriars, Trafalgar Square, the Tate, *and* the Royal Exchange.

A WAITER CALLED ARTHUR

I stayed at my old hotel, and the lift was out, the hot water a tepid mockery, the food unfit for stray cats in Los Angeles. The English could never cook, but now they have nothing to cook with. It was a good place for me to catch up with my ideas of losing ten pounds. Even Covent Garden and its cabbage stalls looked poorly.

Arthur, the old waiter, remembered me. "It's good to see you, sir," he said. "I'm leaving, you know, for Canada. Going to chop down trees, haul lumber, and grow some blasted wheat."

"At your age, Arthur?"

"I got two lads and the missus is fairly active—'usky blood lines, you know. Care for creamed fish?"

"No, any kippers?"

"Not a scale. Can't even get you anything on the sly from a spiv. They keep the black market down. Only the rich get anything on it."

"What would you advise?"

"Get invited out to dinner. The tea here isn't bad. No sugar, I remember you take it plain—no cream or milk."

"What's at the music hall?" I asked.

Arthur smiled showing his Labour Party teeth and his eyes lit up behind his Free Medical Plan glasses, "Now you're talkin'. The Knockout Four and the Blackpool Boys."

We shared a common interest in music-hall turns, and in low Cockney comics. We planned a night out in the 'alls, but

A MUSIC-HALL TURN

Turtle called and said I was to come right out to the studios. I got a cab—one of the new ones, not one of the relics that look as if they took George IV to Bath—and drove out to London's Brooklyn where most of the studios were.

Turtle had a big desk and enough relatives and bowers around him to make me think of Hollywood. I told them what I planned to film, and we ran off Fisher's film shots. Then we sat around and it ended up in me promising to write an outline called a "treatment" for the musical picture about a trip around the world.

I said to Turtle, "I can't work in London, I'll starve to death."

One of the bright young men said, trying to sound as much like Aldous Huxley as he could, "We have a company shooting up north—a Hitchcock-type thriller, why not go up there? Some food up there. Bixley got half a cheese last week."

Turtle sat up. "He did?"

"Used it to seduce that Hungarian dancer."

Turtle relaxed. "The swine! Haven't had a bit of good cheese myself for some time." He turned to me. "Will you try it up there? You should have it done in a few weeks. How do they say it in Hollywood?"

I said, "We say, 'Take your time, and have it Tuesday.'"

Nobody laughed. But they never do at American jokes . . .

NORTH OF ENGLAND

7   the unstately homes of England

I WAS very happy in Wales—writing Turtle's musical picture—on the Tawry River, above Llangadock. Artist country, village mine, and rock country. There was only one phone—in a pub—so Turtle couldn't reach me.

Then I went away to a Wales town in the Cambrian Hills where no one knew me, to a mountaintop where a summer orchestra sawed Bach on damp fiddles while the drummer fought the summer gnats among the voices of artistic Londoners trying to say Llandifawnswansca as if born to it. I made some progress on the screenplay.

The Cambrians, low hills and mountains, blue gorges turning mysteriously green, are not like any other hills, and the warm worn brick, the clapboard doors weathered to sil-

63

ver, the small green fields and the great oaks in a silk curtain of rain are very dear to me—when they do not bore me. The land seems to breed a serene, impartial numbness on the mind. They feed off rare beef and a fair soup of beef bones and oats, and drink a very dark ale. It was certainly better than starving in London.

I lived at an old house and ate whatever the village and farm and my people ate, and I walked once a day to the town for the newspaper, and once a day for the mail. (I could have done it all in one walk but I detest efficiency in anything but the arts.) I wrote, almost by direct intuition, a motion picture about fun on a world's tour. Hedges of barberry, whittlehorn, and woodbine were along the wet road, and my shoes—heavy farm shoes—very dry.

A CAMBRIAN NATIVE

In the evening I sat on the front steps watching the night insects bump noses around the one dim light, and after a while I would crawl into my bed and sleep long hours, in which I dreamed long, odd, and pleasant dreams that I forgot on rising. Mornings smelled of fennel and fine, fat kippers on the fire, of Scot oatmeal and lean, black Irish bacon and a bitter India tea, and of sweet cicely, dill, and thyme soaked into preserves and smoked meats.

I read very little. I had lost the habit of devouring books by the dozen. A few worn favorites, the few shreds of an education, still clung to me. I kept writing.

When the prowling fall winds came wolfing down through the worn fence rails and the muskrat and otter put on winter fat—and the morning hours were chill and heavy with cold, I finished the job and fled to London like lichens hunting a favorite stone. London was shabby; blanched ladies busy repainting old faces; the prigs of the new group in power; the bald foreheads of the leaders; the same poor . . .

THE BIG AMERICANS

Turtle read it and said, "I like it."

"You sound as if I dared you to."

"Now the people who are putting up the money for the film—go talk to them. Go visit the Big Americans."

I had no pride. I wired the Big Americans and asked if I could come to American House for a few days. I knew them and wondered why they were backing motion pictures.

American House in Kent had not changed, wild honeysuckle and green-berried sumac still grew along its paths.

The Big Americans (not to be confused with the Little Americans who were exporters of scotch) were a family who dealt in old paintings, and I loved them all dearly.

Betty was my favorite. She was young, beautiful, and always hungry. Living among classic art dealers had made her beautiful.

She was watching me closely after dinner and her breath blubbered before she controlled it. "It's a time of big things."

"Times are bad and getting worse," I said.

"Not that."

I gave her a stare. There was a new, sleek complacency about her, like a flamenco singer in a popular night club.

"What's up, Betty?"

"You know Mac?"

"Yes, I know Mac. Say—"

"I'm going to marry him."

BETTY OF THE BIG AMERICANS

She looked me over with care and sank into a chair. "That is, I might. A woman ought to have a home, a husband. 'Home is where you go and they have to let you in,' some poet said. Well, I want that kind of a home, not a barroom or a *maison de passe* every night, full of London freaks who say witty things."

"You love Mac?"

"Shucks, yes."

"It's an odd world, Betty."

"You worry, too."

"Sure."

"Well," she brushed my cheek with one of her long eye-lashes, "civilization has always tottered—onward."

We let it go at that.

I suppose Mac is a great man. I met him for the first time, after reading Stendhal's *Le Rouge et le noir,* and I regret I can't write of him as he should be written of. (How fine it would be if one could write in slow motion so that we could see all actions slowed down as clear as the mysterious, still shyness of small, wild animals.)

MAC THE MONSTER

Mac had been born in India, the son of an American missionary at some hill station, into a family that had been missionaries for a hundred years. There was nothing for or against his people except that they were poor and too earnest, and that they secretly loved the natives whom they brought in great numbers to God (when the crops failed). Mac loved his mother and father, and when he was a great man he walked down Fifth Avenue or Downing Street—someone used to say—as if parading a dead parent on each arm.

Mac was the bright one of the litter.

Having lost faith at college, but not hope, he came down

to the Harvard Club and saw that the gentlemen who controlled the world were the kind of people he admired. Not for their money but for their clean houses, their clean look, their honest love of what they had. He admired everything that was clean, that was honest, that was old and settled. He grew sick to see around him the persistent betrayal of college idealism.

He went into partnership with a native talent who had a fine mind but weak lungs, and they began to write reports for many holding companies, explaining how fine and wonderful banking is. They were honest partners and did honest work, and by the time the partner died ("of a hard peace between two simple, savage wars"), someone said Mac was a great man. He was a director of missions, of holding companies, he converted Red writers to the advertising business, he owned a great fortune, and he was a missionary for good in anything to which you could attach a stock issue. He was honest and admitted that he had a mind, and even here he was not talking from mere ego; he saw honestly the great empty heads, the hollow heads all around him. He developed tender, social antennae of great length that extended into Nice, Rome, Santa Barbara, Madrid, and Palm Beach.

He married coldly and with the best of taste into a First Family—he spawned some pale children who shook hands with visitors wearing white gloves, and sounded like their English governess. But love he distrusted, for it was, "like modern poetry—a pain in the eye."

In the end he left his wife (she developed a wonderful, mature case of arteriosclerosis as a replacement) and his great enterprises and came to London to try to figure himself out. He tried to recapture the sensibility of boyhood while drunk. He spoke a broad A, but slipped into news-magazine style when drunk, and helped exiled Poles. He never used the word *lived* in his whole life, *life* was a better word to him, and he avoided, he told me once, "the fingers of furtive women."

He was very unhappy and hunted for the fine passionate feel‧
ing of the very young.

A MODERN ROMANCE

Then he met Betty at a tea for Royal Greek Exiles and she
grinned at him, and suddenly he saw that he had lived all his
life with too many noble syllables. For the first time his day
rang like a tapped goldfish bowl. He patted down his thinning
left-handed hair part and lowered his Cro-Magnon chin and
fell into what he knew was a wonderful escape from his loss
of faith in life. He wanted only a cause. Betty would be
a cause. Or would be as long as she was cool and socially
accepted; for his world was made up of honest mottoes and
very fine patterns and he hated to think of the dirt and evil in

A TEA FOR ROYAL GREEK EXILES

the world. He could never even stay in a hotel—he once said—where "the plumbing bubbled in the night."

I met him the next day at a lunch given for Hungarians who had left Budapest in a hurry.

Mac opened his mind to us over an afternoon scented with a formal tea, as the day died quickly in the windows. And I saw that he was hunting sanctuary, even when not pursued. I found out he was really behind Turtle and his films.

"It's time," Mac told me, "someone with intelligence and taste made films."

"Yes, it is," I said. I wasn't impressed because I have heard this line a hundred times. And nothing much ever happens. Hollywood goes on making the films, the same films.

"I'm in this thing to show that films are an art form."

"They can be," I admitted.

"If they're not art, what are they?"

"Entertainment. You can't make art films and make money."

"I've made all my money."

"But you can lose it, too, in art films."

Mac shook his head. "I have the touch. I have never lost money. I've done everything and now I want to make films. Turtle is a very smart producer. What's the matter with his liver?"

"I think it's just producer's stomach. His ulcers have ulcers."

"Oh. And I feel he's right in this round-the-world film idea. I'm backing him. I'm paying your salary."

"So I gather. I'm not so sure this film will make money. You haven't got a director for it yet?"

"I'll get the best when we're ready."

"I hope you're right," I said. "I've seen too many of these films never get made."

Mac shook his head. "Don't worry."

"I'm not," I said. I wasn't. It seemed very foolish with international crises and trouble all over the world to worry over a musical film. Mac interested me more than his film. He was a new kind of world citizen; beyond taxes, political systems, good or evil, or faith in anything but himself. The world was full of them, I knew. Mac was just the best washed.

8   the suffering of the rich

IN THE end Mac went to Paris to head an order of a Wonderful Group of Fine People—and they seemed to think that he was still married to his first wife—and as she was a First Family and a power in the Wonderful Group, he didn't marry Betty. He went back to his first wife and her practically priceless collection of T'ang china. He wasn't happy, but he was useful according to his code. But I'm getting ahead of my story . . .

After dinner that night, I was listening to a wireless concert when Betty came downstairs and into the living room. She seemed very calm, not cold or sleek or solidly sure of herself, as I had expected her to be. Her face was slackly molded but she was not fatigued.

She sat down facing me, gently, almost unobtrusive.

"Betty . . . how are you?"

She had her little black cigarettes with her. She lit one.

"*You* Americans," Betty said.

"You, too . . . you're tarred with the Yankee brush."

"I guess so. Why do we stay here? Me, Mac, you, Dad . . . everyone."

"Where?"

"Here in Europe."

"Why?" I asked.

"Yes."

"Maybe we're snobs, Betty. Like Henry James in Sussex, Gert Stein on the Rue de Fleuris, Hemingway in Pamplona . . ."

"*That* Ernest," Betty waved her arm.

"Whistler on Battersea Bridge, T. S. Eliot in his cathedral."

Betty kept on waving. "Too easy . . . snobbery isn't the answer."

"Tom Wolfe at Havels in Berlin drinking *Pfalzer*, Ezra Pound, the ex-towel boy from Rome . . . the Air Hero at Goering's and . . ."

"To hell with denouncing expatriates. Just tell me why . . . why we come, why we stay?"

"Ever read Van Wyck Brooks?"

"No."

"He said: 'Magnificent pretensions. Pretty performances! The fruits of an irresponsible imagination, of a deranged sense of values, of a mind working in the void, uncorrected by any clear consciousness of human cause and effect' . . ."

"He said that about me?"

"No, about Henry James . . ."

I shut off the wireless and we had a brandy each. The vast, dark obscurity of the night gripped us. She sat very still and we could see the white line of the surf on the coast, and hear

EVER READ?

the rocking buoys tolling, and smell the wild grapes and hemlock. The house was cool—it had not yet awakened from its season's sleep.

Below there was a chrome-yellow smudge in the night; a boat, far off, passing, its lights like a badly spilled yolk on the blue pan of the sky. A whistle blew somewhere. Was this England in the middle of the twentieth century?

Betty said suddenly, "It's a very old house. I used to think of it as my house. I used to think I would be a great lady here some day . . . When I was small I had an aunt who used to come here often, and I used to help brush her long hair when we had parties at night. And I was allowed to sit on the stairs behind the potted poinsettias and peep at the important people of the world below me.

"That's how I remember the smell of my aunt's long chestnut hair, the crackle of the pearl-handled comb in it, the odor of her body powder—she had beautiful arms and she powdered them before every party."

"They used to," I said. "Betty, why don't you go back to America? You belong there."

"When I came back from school, my aunt was dead . . . very quickly, they said. And the roof leaked in the blue wing."

"There is a French boat leaving tomorrow. You have a passport?"

"Did you ever live in an old house? Smell it, feel it, taste it? Every mouse nest, every layer of wallpaper is full of generations, the family, the people who lived there before us. I think we have too many layers of wallpaper here. But I loved it very much. I shall always remember it as I liked it best. The candles lit, the hired music playing tunes as soft as Bavarian cream. And the guests hurrying across the lawn . . . and my aunt letting me comb out her long hair. Hair doesn't smell that way any more."

"Better get some sleep."

VOICES IN AN OLD HOUSE

"Things don't die and pass because they once happened. They are always there. For only the past is honestly real, the present is nothing until we can look back on it. My aunt will always be here, warm, alive; and I shall always be combing her long hair. She will never die, except to the doctors who were there . . . I shall always be that little, dreaming girl . . . I shall always be the palpably honest child . . . am I nuts?"

"I don't think so. There is a theory of time in which all the events of the past and of the future, too, have all happened and are strung each like a bead on a string. Who are we to say that all the beads are not all there—all happened at once this very moment?"

"That's right . . . everything is happening . . ."

"It's like what that man Einstein speaks of—throwing a stone into space from a moving train. Perhaps he can throw it also into time. Then, all that matters is where you stand. From where you see the stone fall or see the event happen."

IN AN OLD HOUSE

"You're trying to fill me full of a long-haired theory . . ."

I just sat there, very still. Torn clouds had gathered around a tattered moon. After a time, her voice, very husky and low, spoke. It is strange how memorial intimacies, even those that never happened, can be communicated by a voice in the dark —precise emotions.

"Mac will never marry me. I'll leave for Paris tomorrow— catch that boat."

"Good. You'll like America."

"See me to the boat," Betty said.

The old house creaked at times like a wooden sailing ship at sea. And there were the old smells of a well-lived house. But of course it meant little to me, for I hadn't grown up in it. I wondered if I were advising Betty properly.

The sky colored that wonderful lilac color, like the inner skin of a plum, and the cloud that had hovered all night over the house moved out into the sea and dissolved into a perfect crayon-blue. Just at that time, and only for a moment, the coming day smelled like old letters burning . . .

RETURN TO PARIS

Paris was wet and yet glowing. Betty seemed excited and happy. She was dressed in deep blue with a smart little hat and a trim veil across her face. A tremendous raindrop, big as a grape, fell. The sudden rain made a Fête des Ombrelles of the streets . . .

"Thank you for your help," she said.

"You will find your tickets in this envelope, Betty."

"Good-by," she said, and the last I saw of her, she was following a porter loaded with much pigskin luggage, down toward her train, and one of the yellow tearoses had shredded and was dropping petals onto the dirty stone floor of the station . . . (I used this scene in a novel I was writing, but it didn't come out right.)

When her train left, shaking the station as it unwound itself for the spring, the wild leap, across the countryside, I knew suddenly that it was intrinsically probable I might never see her again.

Thinking it over, how many thousands of people I shall never see again!

The train was gone. And when it was gone and the dust no longer fluttered in the vibrations of its passing, I could still

IN THE STATION WAITING ROOM

hear it, far off, pounding along at great speed, frequently, persistently shouting.

Then that, too, stopped. The dust rested—floated like golden pollen in the station air. The station clock stirred its longest hand just a little in space, and a fat man passed, quickly feeding himself salted nuts out of a paper bag with insatiable gluttony . . . and I had a feeling inside me that kept saying: "The orchard is sold, they are cutting down the cherry trees in a Russian play . . ."

There was the smell of hot grease and pigeon droppings. The great glass top of the station grew bluer and darker. Two lovers passed, holding hands, discreetly anxious. A little man knee-deep in bundles, seated in apathetic silence, looked at

the clock, then went back to ruminating among his bur-
dens . . .

In a way there is a happy ending. Betty has opened an an-
tique shop in Beverly Hills and is doing very well. Her letters
are long and happy (someday I shall rewrite that novel about
her) . . .

Meanwhile Turtle was screaming for me to return and pro-
ceed with the film. He had lots of Mac's money and I had no
regrets in spending it.

SOUTH OF FRANCE

9   the grab bag of Europe

TURTLE took me to his club for lunch. The food was fair and skimpy.

"Returning to Europe," he said, "is like coming back from a rocket journey to the moon or Mars, Stevie. One lands again in a populated country, on a seashore that is familiar, yet one senses almost at once the great fear and feels like the Fattened Calf, this time for a change, hunting the Prodigal Son."

"I'm hungry, Turtle, not sad."

"I feel for Europe sorrow and affection today."

"It's sinister and yet dull," I said.

"An empty life is the perfect definition of happiness, old boy. Simplified morality is the best. It consists of staying out of jail and wedlock and approaching life with an attitude that scared the Sabine women."

"Let's have some whisky."

I suppose Turtle is right, but I do not belong to his school of thought. I still feel and touch, and see and hear, and the cage of Europe jars me. Turtle may be right; inertia may be the true animal level; that would explain why all saints seem dull.

I left him and a week later got Fisher, my cameraman, and left for the south of France to film more scenes for the movie.

Flying over Europe was looking down on the twisted remains of cities, bridges; peering down on the great roads white as dead bones in the sun.

Turtle had flown ahead to pick up stuff to shoot.

FRANCE—THE VINEYARDS

As we passed over the mountains to the south of France, I could not see it merely as an innocent passer-by. I was not innocent and I had been there before. The great hillsides were green in vineyards, the smoking manure heaps still bravely guarded the doorways of the farmhouses, and someone had put out more flags and hired a band, and even as our plane came in, a wedding procession started on a dusty back road. I was pleased to see, by the footprints, that even the priest had taken of the wine. And spotted coach dogs followed the procession, their tongues out . . . the French don't really change much.

ON THE BLUE SEA

The plane landed with a thud. The Mediterranean sun made every shadow black as India ink, and the egg-yolk-colored sidewalks seemed to burn like heated brass. Turtle came across the airfield waving his cane and as he pumped my hand, he said:

"You look really terrible."

"I feel fair. It's good to be back to the Riviera."

"Don't be too sure, old boy. Cap d'Antibes isn't what it once was, and never has been. But it's very good to film. Rich people, poor people, and all kinds of scandal . . . Fisher, you have enough film?"

"Yes, Mr. Turtle."

We went down to the bar at the Pavilion of the Eden Roc and looked at the bathers. The women were wearing the fashionable French excuse for a bathing suit, and the men were all brown and healthy looking until they came up to the bar and showed their yellow eyeballs and the nervous twitch in their throats. They opened their Paris *Herald* with an easy roll of the wrist, took a deep suck on their drinks before they read anything.

"What's it like here?" I asked Turtle.

"Crazy. We sit here on the white rock of the Cap. Cannes fifteen minutes away in one direction, and Monte an hour that-a-way, son."

It's considered very vulgar to call Monte Carlo anything but Monte. I looked out over the pale beige walls and the big rocks and the mansard roofs and the place didn't look as if any change had taken place. But somehow I could feel the change (like with a woman who has suddenly changed her perfume). Eden Roc, its gravel paths, its pine trees, its big umbrellas, its sun-colored drunks, its little children and their starched nurses and brandy-loaded mothers, *all* looked as I remembered them as an art student.

Still the people were different people, the smart countess wasn't a countess any more; the White Russian exiles were Poles now and remembered the cheerful, prewar pogroms of their fatherland instead of the glory of the tsar's St. Petersburg. The whole Côte d'Azur was in the grip of a deadly panic, and the panic consisted, Turtle said, of people who were "not going to talk about the panic, damn it, not one peep."

They spoke of love, gowns, the Lloyd's Bank at Monte, the Palm Beach Casino at Cannes, and 100,000-franc plaques at the Big Table, or who had cut whom dead in the Carlton in Cannes, and weren't the *concierges* and maîtres d'hôtel all turning into Reds? *L'homme propose, et Dieu dispose.*

The food, as Turtle proved to me, was as it had always been. The champagne, a *vin du pays rosé,* caviar, soufflés, and *mille feuilles.* I let him pick up the bar chits to show I was a loyal employee, and borrowed the use of his *cabaña,* after letting him beg me hard to take it—the time it took me to finish one solid, nourishing martini.

"What gives? Can we film what we like?"

Turtle looked over a near-nude female bather and groaned.

ON THE BEACH

"Cannes, Juan-les-Pins, Antibes, Nice, all have Socialist-Communist municipal councils."

"How does it work?"

"Fine. They encourage us to spend madly so they can keep the country floating. Every time I play baccarat in the worst luck, I buy milk for a hundred poor French kids. Ah, how the neat piles of 100,000-franc chips fly and how the cows of France must suffer and be tugged on, all because of our film company."

"What else is going on?"

"You are an old friend of the Candy Blossom?" asked Turtle. "We're shooting scenes at her villa."

"I'm not an old friend," I answered. "I knew Candy Blossom years ago when I was writing for radio shows. She was then the pretty stooge for a fast-talking comic."

"How was she?"

"She was very funny, but they were both fired from radio. The comic went to Hollywood. And she decided to collect diamond bracelets."

"That's the Candy Blossom."

MY FRIEND MISS BLOSSOM

Candy Blossom was not the lady's real name, but then no one ever remembered her real name. She was a very kind creature with some vague southwestern "you-all-magnolia-blossom" background, and she had been a small actress of smaller parts before she decided to collect bracelets. Now she was the postwar popularity winner of the south of France. "Knee-deep in Argentines," as she used to say. And her diamond bracelet collection was up to her elbows, but as she said, "Honey chile, my arms git longer all the time . . . I'm one tomato that always has room for one more."

Candy Blossom was really the American ambassador of good will in her own way. "She does much less harm," Turtle said, "than former Ambassador Bullitt, Danny Kaye, or visiting senators."

Turtle looked down at his *oeufs à la neige* in a mousse of coffee (he was always a romantic about desserts) and said, "Candy Blossom is charging us by the day to use her villa."

"I'll have Fisher shoot fast."

"We can get our money back reselling the American rights. She cut quite a row in America?"

"To quote her, she 'mowed 'em down!' "

"Good. Go get those shots."

"She sleeps till noon," I said. "The play very big at the tables this year?"

"Not as big as it used to be. But with Monte only fifty kilometers away, one manages to get rid of one's extra expense money quickly. The food holds up well. Know the Bonne Auberge?"

"Between Antibes and Nice? Scott Fitzgerald beat up a sailor there once."

Turtle bowed his head in homage to Scotty over his drink. "We shall never see the likes of Scotty again in our time. Good writer, too . . . Then there is the Château Madrid near Monte. They really know what to do with a black-market suckling pig."

"What does it cost?"

"Like the very devil. Six thousand francs a person. Sixty dollars in your blasted, easy-to-get, American money."

I ignored our European loans. No one loves us for them.

I looked out across the Golfe Juan. This was a place I had known well. Now it was all desperate people, Europe's scum; broken-winded aristocrats, Belgian *nouveau riche*. And Americans, who were not any more artists, painters, tennis bums, or gamblers, but Americans with tax-free fortunes, all citizens of Monte; generals full of aircraft graft, supply-dump majors or haters of Roosevelt and Truman—criminals, the war rich, the jaded bits of psychiatrists' bait. American hostesses with Kansas fortunes; Belgian black-market kings; Swiss smugglers; Nazi-loving Swedes; and, as usual, the Argentines, who had all the beef in the world to sell—for cash. It hadn't changed so much after all, I decided.

I REMEMBER GARBO

There weren't many of the *congés payés* left, the little French clerk or salesman who once came here for two weeks

with his fat wife, his fat dog, and his leggy kids to store up
enough sunshine for a whole year in a damp Paris flat. Prices
were too high. Everyone tried hard for a certain *fin-de-siècle*
grandeur, and if not as many people blew their brains out as
used to, it was because bullets cost a hundred francs each.
One could only sit on the terrace and shudder at the old faces
looking older than ever; faces like old hawks caught in the
sun with their age etched in the wrinkles of pea-green faces.

"Such a crowd of faces," said Turtle, pointing them out.
Elsa Maxwell, the old sea lioness herself, lifting a chaos of
features into a teacup; Sir and Lady Bindle, the brittle creak
of their aged bones like the sound of the decaying palm fronds
rubbing each other overhead. And the vice-polished mask of
wine merchants, old actors, ladies of sacred and profane
memories. And the cash-register eyes of Schiaparelli, "Scap,"
moving from group to group with some new, shrill nonsense
about fashions, modes, styles, and fabrics. Jack Warner from
Hollywood smelling of cigars.

The surf was filled with Queensboroughs, Paleys, the
spawnings of the Aga Kahn. Under the palms was Chevalier
and a gum-chewing Garbo, like a gray shadow under a rancid
straw hat, the surgeon's slit of a mouth saying nothing, the
big feet in flat-heeled shoes scuffing the dust in front of the
Cannes Casino. And always the suntanned, the oiled, anointed,
and scraped, shaved, scented, muscled flesh.

"Only the sunlight is free," said Turtle, "and on a clear
day one can see Orson Welles, and wonder if God was still
only watching sparrows fall."

"I don't like it any more, Turtle," I said suddenly, getting
up.

"It was a great place once, old boy. But we were younger."

"Not only that. We weren't in a hurry. All these people now
act as if in ten minutes someone were going to take them out
and shoot them."

"Perhaps they are. They're waiting for the first atom bomb, second series."

"I'll go get the camera set up."

ONLY THE SUNLIGHT IS FREE

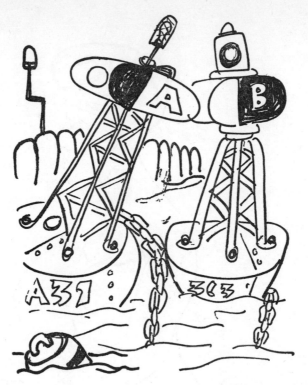

FRENCH COAST

10   a character called Candy

CANDY BLOSSOM'S villa faced the sea. She was seated on a cane sofa, wearing her bracelets and finishing her own lunch of pâté of duck *baguette*, some *baguettes* of bread at her jeweled elbow. She remembered the radio shows, the old days in New York and the simple saga of her days as an actress. She didn't mind talking—she was writing the story of her life. She explained she had, "no relatives, only friends."

"Good."

"*Houston to Heaven*, how's that for a title?"

MISS CANDY BLOSSOM

"It's not bad," I said.

"It's a jim dandy, honey boy, just a jim dandy. But how would *The Granddaughter of Scarlett O'Hara* sound?"

"Scarlett is a fictional character."

"I've been called that, too."

"How does the writing go?"

"Oh, slow. I've sharpened all my pencils . . . and I have a wonderful magnolia-colored paper to write on."

"You haven't really started yet?"

"It's the spelling, honey boy. All them men called D'Harcourton, De Noailliess, Piccarolla, Amerigo Gentillinni, Pierro Gueefii, de Breteuil (he raised a mighty fine hounddog), Chavchavadze, Mike Royamount (he's got that Eyetalian car long as a tape worm), Scala Bernensonn." She looked at me and shook her head. "The spelling gives me a headache."

"What about simple guys, like John Smith?"

"I haven't seen *that* Elk in years."

"I just made up that name."

"No, you didn't. I remember him. The son of a D.A.R.!"

"I didn't mean him."

"That spelling is going to kill this little ole tomato. Know a good publisher?"

"I can get you an offer for your life story."

Candy Blossom stood up and yawned. She yawned all over, scratched her jeweled wrists, and said, "Let me think it over. What's my take?"

"A big down payment, and a part of the profits."

"A girl has to think of her old age. A large down payment, and they can keep their ole cut of the profits."

"I'll write them."

Candy Blossom dipped a golden apricot in some honeycomb honey and sighed. "Boy, when I was throwing bad jokes to Jocko, the comic, I never expected to own a villa here and almost break my arm wearing all this trash."

"Times change."

"I never liked working on the stage. You know why?"

"Why?" I asked.

"It's so g.d. vulgar."

THERE ARE POOR FRENCHMEN

We shot scenes of the villa the whole afternoon. Fisher was not much of a human being, but he could use a camera and the light was right and he liked the way clouds were formed. Cameramen, I found out, don't care for much in life besides good clouds.

After the day's work, I ducked out on Turtle and Fisher

and went down to little place near the big dock and sat drinking wine. It was not fancy here and nobody was rich and you could smell the bedding, and the men hadn't shaved for three days.

Sometimes I get confused—it's not hard for me—and I feel things are unreal, but in a little place, not too clean but well lit and smelling of wine and garlic, is a good way to come back.

A tall, lean Frenchman came over and sat down by me. "I hear you make movie. I one damn fine boy."

"You an actor?"

"No. In French underground, in war, I help film roads and

ONE OF THE FIGHTING FRENCH

things. I mark out highways for Red Ball Express. The trucks with the big black men driving petrol for the Army tanks. I'm pretty good to have around."

"I'm sorry, we have a cameraman. How are things here?"

"For hunger. I used to fish, but it's no good, the prices they pay. I'm a guide now. You like anything? You can't shock me, I can get it for you."

"No, I have everything. Have a brandy."

"I thank you."

"It's all right. Tell me about the underground."

"All lies, no matter what you hear. Some were brave, some were not. But mostly all lies. It was really nothing. Some died, some got rich," he swallowed his drink.

"You a Red?"

"*Merde*, no. I'm for me. Everybody in Europe is."

ONE MORE PARTY

The next night I worked. Turtle had arranged to film a party of a "Princess" introducing her daughter into society—local society. Some were the archbishop's friends. Some were rich because their grandfathers had been rich—some were poor. Some looked very well in the pages of the French *Vogue*. It was the kind of an affair that is called "in the Faubourg St.-Germain tradition," which meant that a tent for dancing had been erected over the neglected garden and several people sang to plucked-guitar accompaniment. Faded feathers, tiaras, aigrettes, torn red velvet, and peeling gilt had mixed into an atmosphere when I got there. Fisher had the camera and lights set up.

The Princess X could claim such ancient forefathers as Saint Louis, the King of Navarre, Cardinal Richelieu, *and* the trap drummer in a jazz band that came out of the Congo in 1912 and took Paris by storm. The thing that I admired about

THE PRINCESS X

the Princess *X* was that she was just as proud of the trap drummer as the cardinal. She used to say, "*fais ce que dois, advienne que pourra!*"

I was standing under the patched tent watching the dancing when someone said, "This spit-queen champagne isn't for this little ole tomato. It gives me rubber legs. Ducky, get me some brandy."

I turned around. There was Candy Blossom on the arm of an aging French senator—a charming crook. I bowed to her and she bowed back and winked, and the senator went off to get her some brandy.

"How is the life story coming?" I asked.

"Terrible. I gave it up, honey boy. That cute little guy is two chapters in it alone and how the h. am I going to write about it? He's called—hold on, honey—he's called Hervé Claude Alphandssee Sereulles Gouin. That's only part of it. Besides," she rattled her jewel-crusted arms, "taking him out is easier than writing. He personally owns every third bunch of grapes in France. And they *all* drink wine here!"

It was a very respectable party otherwise—the shabby people not ashamed of their stains and wear and tear.

Fisher hated it and said, "You can hear the tumbrels rolling."

He got angry when I asked him what a "tumbrel" was.

11   Picasso

THE Riviera town of Antibes has changed a great deal, more than most places. Invaded, exploited by audacious tastes in amusement, full of the scarred surface manifestations of life in Europe today, even the old castle Grimaldi used as a museum has become a sounding board for new doctrines of art. Fisher wanted to film Picasso at work. He was painting in the old castle.

Some of Antibes hadn't changed—the shabby palms, the too-blue sea, and the maternal claw of French nurses pulling small fry from the shoreline to drain them publicly of excess moisture.

We were waiting for permits to go back to Berlin. Turtle wanted shots of night life.

I went to a café called Hôtel des Voyageurs that had *élan* and butter, and red-bordered mirrors like a *maison close.* Even a *tzigane* band with a cymbal player. The old, unhappy-looking waiter came over and said in a surly voice I was welcome and *"enfin,"* he had no suggestions to make. It was all *"cuisine bourgeoise* and filling." Things were very bad all over. He rubbed his *framboise*-colored nose and said, "Why are waiters always supposed to be such characters? I'm not a character. I hate the work. Times are hard and I'm still supposed to be a character."

"I don't know, I'm sure," I said, ordering the veal and a bottle of Malmsey.

"Qui est ce phénomène—là?"

"Yes. Tell me, is Picasso around here much?"

"The painter chap? Yes. He cost me a thousand francs last week."

"Doesn't he tip?"

"Damn it, how was I to know he was a famous mug! He comes in here looking like anybody else—a tailor, an *agent de La Sûreté*—anybody at all. I serve him and he draws a lot of doodles on the hard biscuits—stuff my grandson can do better. He leaves and I toss the biscuits to the doorman's dog. The brute will eat anything. Now the doorman is furious at me. Livid with rage, the sod."

"The dog died?"

"No. The doorman, who has been here a long time, sells these biscuits, drawn on by this fellow, for five thousand francs! People frame these damn biscuits!"

He beat off some flies with a copy of the *Paris-Soir.* "Damn these artistic prowlers into society!"

"On hard biscuits?" I asked.

"Oh, yes. *Ca c'est très intéressant."* A spotted coach dog

THE WAITER

with greedy eyes and ropy ears came in and the waiter looked at him.

"Look," said the waiter, "the dog in residence here. A walking art gallery. He is full of original Picassos."

I could understand the waiter's anger. Nothing is wasted in Europe these days, not even art.

AN INTERVIEW WITH AN ARTIST

After dinner I went to the Grimaldi Museum. I was happy to see the admission was thirty francs—no longer five— Picasso was drawing the crowd, and the castle was taking advantage of it. There will always be a France.

The new paintings, framed only in thin, dark borders, were gay, loud, simple and pure Picassos. Watermelons, goats, pots, shepherds, fishermen—all were clear, fine things that looked as if the models had practical sex lives.

A balding man with a fringe of white hair, a great deal of sunburned flesh, very large, expressive eyes, and beautiful toes in open-toed sandals came in and looked at the paintings. It was Pablo Picasso in old age. It was over ten years since I had seen him last. He had aged, grown more compact, complex, almost shorter.

He fumbled a cigarette into his mouth and I offered to light it. He thanked me and we talked a little while professionally about painting. He did look shorter, stockier, but his legs were very muscled. He looked encased in art like a beetle in amber.

I asked if I could sketch him while we talked. He gestured, grimaced, smiled.

"Why not?"

"Lots of people ask you what you think of art today?"

He shrugged his shoulders and blew out a great deal of tobacco smoke.

"Why talk of what we do? Everyone who wants to can see it—if he wants to."

I agreed everyone talked too much about art and looked very little at it.

"Are you still changing your styles?"

"Changes in manner are not to me an evolution or steps to some unknown idea of painting. I paint for the present— and I paint it so it will always remain for the present."

"Is painting getting better?"

"In the history of art some periods are more positive than others. In other words, sometimes some artists are better than other artists."

I couldn't ask for anything fairer. I said so and we shook hands and blinked in the sun and smoked.

"*Ah, oui, alors.*"

"Good-by . . ."

I was impressed by Picasso, as usual, and I wrote out my notes of his talk at once. I have few heroes but he was still a force in art. Solid, older, true—as who wasn't? But he painted bolder and better than ever. There is no use explaining his work by words alone. Art should be seen, not written about. How many foolish books had been written about art; I do not desire to add to the nonsense. It is like feeding the hungry toothpicks.

I went back to my hotel singing "*Princesses, Duchesses, et Marquises,*" and found a wire from Paris:

> MISS TONE OUR PHOTOGRAPHER IN BERLIN PLEASE CONTACT HER WHEN YOU GET THERE AS WE DO NOT HEAR FROM HER.

It was signed by a fashion magazine editor's name I had once worked for and I wondered what could have happened to Miss Tone, that tall girl a little mad over cameras.

I know it is romantic to talk about the Iron Curtain, but this is nonsense. I was sure Miss Tone was in no sinister danger.

At the airport I wired Paris I would try to ship Miss Tone home from Berlin. Fisher was gloomy about seeing the Germans again.

Air France still needed new planes.

THE SUPER GOONS

We flew over the Ortler, the Grossglockner, and the Walzman crags. Germany from the air looks almost kind and human and then the still-remaining factories and mills come into sight, and not all are ruined and bombed out. In fact, many of them are still working for the British and the Americans, and the Russians. The kaiser's castle at Kronberg is a big hunk of scenery I noticed as I drank the *Glühwein* the hostess served.

Germany was still the same old Germany, Fisher said, "a

GERMANY IS VERY BUSY

land of super goons very good with tools, very cruel to the human spirit and not at all defeated." There were winter sports as usual at Garmisch-Partenkirchen, and a great deal of good food was stolen from American taxpayers for the black market. The undemocratic arrogance of the German in defeat was as hard to take as always. They still shouted, *"Schmeissen Sie das Schwein 'raus!"*

At Munich the Prinzregenten Theatre was playing Shakespeare, the famous "German" author, as any German in the street will tell you. They did *Hamlet,* and a fat German sat beside me and offered me chocolates from a silver box.

"It is so hard now that the Russians are here. *Gruss Gott!*"

"But so are the Americans and the British and the French."

He tried to bring a tear to a fat eye. "But it is the Russians that are our mutual enemy."

"You are to many," I said, "the enemy they dislike most."

"Ah, *Amerikaner* humor. Have another chocolate," said the fat German. "They come from the British Staff H.Q. I do them secret little favors now and then and they spare me their slops. Poor Germany, what has become of her? Have you been to Bayreuth? American constabulary MPs patroling the sacred Wagnerian groves! *Schweinerei!*"

"Damyankees," I said, "is the proper term."

"*Nein—nein—ein herrliches Nein.* Would you care to join me for dinner? I have entrance to a place. The last little place. Times are so hard for us."

I said yes, I would like to see "a place." I had heard of them.

It was across the street, wide open—a polite *Dummkopf* at the door to open it. In back was a large room in red plush, soft chairs, and a Hungarian orchestra. On the walls pictures of Wagner, Senator Taft, Lady Astor, and Frederick the Great. There was a great deal of food in sight.

The fat German filled my plate with smoked eel, paprika bacon, and some goose liver *truffée.*

"Is this a special place?" I asked.

"But of course. For the old Germans. Calories are fine, but we need food—real food."

"Were you a Nazi?"

"That nonsense? I was of course an *Oberassessor* and Burgomaster for the Nazis with six *Unterassessoren*—but that is over. When do we fight the Russians?"

"Do we?"

He helped me to Hungarian salami and *Emmenthaler* cheese. "You like Moravian sausages and *tvaruzky*?"

"Why do you think we'll use you as Allies?"

"Here is some *salmis de perdreaux*, Westphalian ham."

"I'm not hungry," I said.

"Ah yes, you *have* everything." The fat German took a serving of carp roe and caviar and tried to weep at his misery at having nothing . . . I felt ill and angry.

I turned and went out past a waiter carrying some *salade tartare* and mushrooms in sauce *vinaigrette*. The place was filling up fast with the losers of World War II. They cooked well, but then, as Fisher said, "one doesn't burn six million Jews in furnaces and learn nothing."

THE GERMANS DENAZIFIED

Outside some DPs were going through the sidewalk rubbish and capturing fish heads and valuable potato peelings.

At the corner an American soldier was holding a blonde girl very tight and saying, "Oh, baby—listen, just listen to me, baby—ah, baby—all I keep saying is baby—look, baby."

And the girl laughed and said, "You and your *Gottverdammten* babies. Got money?"

The official currencies are the pound, *Reichsmark*, and American cigarettes. The high comedy was at the Denazification courts where almost any murderer admitted he was never a Nazi; it was always "somebody who looked like me."

We did our night shots.

book 2

THUNDER
IN BOTH EARS

BALLET—BERLIN

12   toe dance macabre

AT THE airport it was cold and a tall girl in a trench coat, carrying two cameras, blew a red nose and held out a gloved hand in greeting. It was Miss Tone, the lady camera-man. She didn't look very lost.

"You lost?" I asked.

"No, why?"

"Your Paris office asked."

"Nuts to them."

"How is the Russian Zone?" I asked her.

"All over . . . every place you look it's still Russia."

"How did they treat you?"

"Seldom. Liquor is hard to get. You like caviar, sturgeon, and hothouse tomatoes?"

"Why not?"

"The hotel has plenty of them, and lots of hot water. Don't tip the help. They don't like it. You interested in politics?"

"No, I'm here making background shots for a movie."

"How about the theater tonight? They're doing the Swan Lake ballet, I think. A Frenchman is taking me. He's cute."

"Don't tell him that."

I didn't have a clear day all through my stay. It rained or was very windy. My chambermaid, red as a strawberry, with big, fat arms, used to look out of the window at the snow whirling around the hotel and sigh.

GERMAN HOTEL MAID

"Such perfect weather."

"A little overcast, no?"

"*Some* rain. What would Germany be without snow?"

"Like California, I suppose."

"You have been to California?"

"I live there."

"In the sun? It does not burn you all up?"

"It's rather nice, you know, sunlight."

"All that yellow stuff, no, thank you. You will be having tea and jam?"

"No, I'm going out, but I could use some cigarettes."

"Four marks a pack."

"I wish they weren't half cardboard tube."

"Tell me, is Gary Cooper really married to Hedda Hopper?"

"I haven't heard."

At the opera the porter asked me if I were an American. I had to admit I was.

"I know Americans. I was in Munich with the Americans. Fine fellows. How are things with your poor country?" he asked.

"Wonderful."

"I hear from the Eastern Zone radio there is a shortage . . . almost no vodka to be had."

"That's true only because . . ."

"And there is, I hear, a shortage of black wolfskin jackets . . ."

"We don't, you see . . ."

"And Tibetan tea, the real black stuff you drink with strong butter. No place serves it at all any more in New York?"

"You are interested in politics?"

"No."

He nodded sadly. "Poor America. No black wolfskin jackets . . . *tut tut*."

"We have plenty of Republicans and second basemen and have you ever eaten a hot dog?"

"By us, Comrade, it is not yet that bad. The dogs are safe."

I gave up.

Miss Tone said, "They're all jerks. I like the U.S.A. What the hell am I doing here?"

"It's a ballet . . . remember?"

ART ON A BIG STAGE

The theater was packed and they were giving not the Swan ballet but Prokofiev's Romeo and Juliet ballet, based on the work of that great "Russian" author, Shakespeare. The accident of his being born to a small, dying Island Empire isn't accepted as a fact making him an Anglo-Saxon.

I enjoyed the show. There is nothing like it in America, not even in Radio City where all I remember of the dull shows is the orchestra coming up out of Hell on a rising elevator; not a very fair substitute for entertainment.

Someone talented danced Juliet, and after that there was a sort of encore with a ballerina who danced the Nutcracker Suite, which a man from the State Department in the next box suddenly discovered was Russian music and not by Walt Disney.

It was a fine show and the customers enjoyed it.

The State Department man who called everybody, male or female, Suh, asked me to join him for a drink in the lobby. There is a drink there called the "cockboy"—which is an American drink, I was told, so I suppose they mean "cowboy." It's vodka, a potato gin, and a raw egg dropped in before your amazed eyes.

We drank it off and Suh looked around him and winked at me.

"Pretty nice girls, Suh?"

"Girls are pretty all over the world."

"Don't you believe it. Spent ten years of my tender youth in London. Very long in the tooth. Spanish tomatoes are very nice, but they don't bathe."

"No?"

"They perfume. Now the Chinese . . ."

I changed the subject. "What do you think of the East Germans?"

"I don't like the leaders."

"How do they like us?"

"They don't like our leaders. What do the French think of us, Suh?"

THE CUSTOMERS ENJOYED IT

"Oh, they like us fine, only they . . ." I stopped and looked at Suh and shrugged my shoulders.

He laughed and ordered two more "cockboys." "Sure, everybody likes everybody else, it's all the leaders' faults. And who are the leaders? People! Some day I'm going to figure out how to run a world without leaders."

"I see your point," Miss Tone said. "It's deep, it's real deep."

"You do?" he said, amazed. "You do?"

"Let me buy the next 'cockboys,' " Miss Tone said.

He said, "If you insist, but you're twisting my arm, forcing me. Vice, you see, is only purity corrupted by direct action."

"One for the road," Miss Tone said.

I looked over the colorful lobby with people getting around "cockboys" and assorted fruit punches.

Miss Tone pointed to a beautiful girl at the bar. "How can one drink cold milk in cold blood?"

I don't remember much more that night.

NO EXPERT REPORTING

It would be very easy for me to become very impressive with words as to what is really going on in Middle Europe. The truth is, I can only give a few personal impressions and leave it at that. I am no expert on economics, politics, or ways of life. I don't know one end of an armored division from the other. I can't explain the Russians, the Germans, or what we are doing in Europe. Maybe it's a great good. Personally, I'm not sure.

Anything I would say of coming events you can do better by looking into your old tea leaves. And reading most of the "experts" on the subject, on both sides, I think that is what they are doing, gazing at old tea leaves.

Miss Tone, after she called her magazine office in Paris, sat down and said it was all simple.

NO EXPERTS ON ECONOMICS

"The way I see it, sport, is like this. People are people, only some are worse people than other people. I don't like arming the kraut-heads. I don't trust them. I don't like the Russians either. And what I think of the French . . ."

"You got stood up?"

She nodded. "I wish I were back in Paris with Alice. Well, I gotta go. I got a date with Fisher. Is he alive?"

"Let me know," I said, and went back to try and knock some sense into the reason for all these background shots in the outline of the script. I was becoming less and less excited about Turtle's motion picture. We were going to join him in Vienna and maybe that would be a good place to tell him his silly movie was no dice.

MARKET IN SEVILLE

13   a very sick Turtle

MOVIE-STUDIO nerves and English food at its postwar level almost killed my friend Turtle. When we got to Vienna, he said, "Take me to a doctor, old boy."

"I know a good one in *Alt Wien*."

Doctor Silbert nodded after he examined him. "Butterflies in the stomach, *ja*?"

He looked at Turtle's stomach through great machines, and in one room they had a mirror that reflected the fluoroscope and we saw a slow, churning, greenish underwater ballet, weird as Dali, and rather exciting. But the doctor said it was nothing.

"Interesting, *nein*? But it shows nothing. See me in a week."

"I feel very ill."

"If you feel worse, come back."

The attacks came back and the doctor suggested Spain as being fine for a rest.

"Spain?" said Turtle. "Say, we could film the wedding of the Duke of A——'s daughter."

"We could," I said. "Miss Tone is covering it for her magazine. She knows the ropes at society weddings."

"Good! Get Miss Tone to meet us at the Spanish border. I'll pay her extra."

"No excitement," said the doctor.

"Who's excited?"

Two days later as we roared down past the cold purple-black hills of France, and as the orange groves first appeared, Turtle lay in his compartment, lamenting his past. I tried to act as if I had butterflies too, and filled the compartment with wild asters and detective novels, for bloodshed in print, Fisher said, is good for the nerves.

It was a pain wave that came up inside Turtle and pressed at his heart and lungs, and a crawling thing seemed to chew inside him, and then when it was over he was sad with no control at all. An attack at Marseilles had come during a lunch by the local film press in our honor.

The local newspaper editor had introduced us to great beefy men who joked of their ulcers and were full of clinical details and cocky, spurious airs. There was even a broker from Majorca in the Balearics who frankly wanted the old days of reaction back and who called it "Roosevelt Stomach" . . . a disease the medical profession is now just writing into history. Turtle was better in the morning and said it was because the brandy was digesting well. He looked sicker to me, but he insisted we go on to Spain.

THE ROAD TO SPAIN

The coast going down toward the border town of Port-Vendres was very heavy with sun—as our hired car ran on. The white rim of sea kept close to the heavy, dark, wet plain of sand. And there was nothing, even in the sky, the clouds were all gone and a new crayon-blue was suddenly carelessly blocked in. Turtle began to talk to me with no pretension of cleverness now; I had developed into a good listener.

He was lonely and maybe he was beginning to see what had happened to him after all these years; something serious was coming into focus. If he wasn't going to die of nerves, he said, and that was silly because the best men in London

FIFTY POUNDS A CONSULTATION

and Paris had looked at his tall, thin, pink, naked body and
rubbed the flesh like lovers (at fifty pounds a consultation)
and had filled his stomach with chalk and photographed it
and all had said it mere nerves. So maybe it was working
too hard.

"Take it easy, Turtle," I said. "It's only studio nerves."

He looked at the thin gold band on his wrist.

"Just habit. I'll be fine in Spain."

We went on to Montpellier, then to Perpignan. We hired
another private car and got ten legal papers to take it down
to Spain with us. Fisher had to list his tools of trade.

Our driver was an Italian from Newark, New Jersey, who
had been deported to Italy as a bootlegger and had managed
to get into France and hire himself out to tourists when
there were tourists. He liked to talk about American crime.

We had a quick, flashing sight of the white ribbon of road,
the heavy undergrowth, months without rain, and the yellow-
ing plants around a watermelon-pink hut. Turtle, who had
not been paying any attention, went back to reading aloud
to me. Turtle found reading aloud helped his nerves. So I
let him read to me.

> The next decades [he read] will be a time of distress
> and gnashing of teeth. We shall live in the hollow of the
> historical wave . . . but the day is not far when the
> present interregnum will end and a new horizontal ferment
> will arise . . . an irresistible global mood, a spiritual
> springtide like early Christianity or the Renaissance. It
> will probably mark the end of our historical era, the
> period which began with Galileo, Newton and Columbus,
> the age of scientific formulation . . . of the ascendance
> of reason over spirit. . . .

"It's not like in New York City," the driver said, "where
a murder could be built up into somethin' sensational. Now
you take the Halls Mills case or Judd Gray—or them people

found in that motorboat driftin' around in Long Island Sound. But out here, I don't know, it just don't add up . . ."

> As the frequency of the convulsions increases [Turtle read], the amplitude of their violence grows; the point of exhaustion has come within almost measurable range. There might be one or two more world wars but not a dozen . . . Meanwhile the chief aim will be to create oases in the interregnum desert . . . In the so-called Dark Ages . . . . such oases assured the continuity of civilization: the monasteries first and later the universities . . . on which no gendarme could set foot . . .

"Maybe it's the frog reporters," went on the driver. "The sun dries their head out and they ain't got the brains or energy to write about murder so it matters . . ."

> We can discern in the past a succession of levels of social awareness, like an ascending staircase. The age of religious wars ended when secular politics began to dominate . . . feudal politics ended when economic factors assumed overriding importance; the struggles of economic man will end by the emergence of the new ethical values of the new age . . . the new movement will reestablish the disturbed balance between rational and spiritual values . . .
>
> In 1917 Utopia seemed at hand. Today it is postponed for the duration of the interregnum. Let us plant oases.

Turtle looked at the landscape. "I hope Miss Tone doesn't get into trouble until we get there. How is Spain these days?"

"For tourists with expense accounts fine," Fisher said. "The sun, good food, and all that very fine, sad music. Like a polite movie jungle, but comfortable, and very exclusive . . . a place where resting is done by tourists who can ignore Franco and his goon squads. Relaxing, but of course not to ridiculous extremes."

FOR TOURISTS IT'S FINE

Turtle said, "It's the food in England got me down."

"Now you take the seafood here . . ." said the car driver.

"You miss America?" I asked.

The driver nodded. "Yeah—deported to the old country. *Porco Dio*."

"Glad to be back here?" I asked.

The man turned to look at us. His eyes were bloodshot and there was a wide gap where two teeth were missing. "Me? No! I'm going to die here. That's why people come back here. To die. Two kinds of people. Those that live here, those that wait down here just to die here. Graveyard in the sun, and the grave bait living in bungalows. This is my old country, they said—Europe. You can have it. I'll never see New-ark again."

The car suddenly ran off the highway and turned toward the sea, where a scribble of masts blinked against a Prussian-blue rock.

The car slowed down at a booth near the border station pier.

A very tall Spaniard in uniform with very red curly hair stood by the blue rock, his scarlet face scalloped with many loose chins . . . The man at the wheel honked twice and the Spaniard smiled in our direction. He looked like a man who was never reduced to compliance and complacency.

THE DRY FIELDS OF SPAIN

He waved a powerful, graceful arm at us.

"Your papers, please."

We handed them over. Turtle said, "We're going to the wedding of the Duke of A———'s daughter."

"Ah, guests."

"Movie people."

The Spaniard waved us on.

Miss Tone, tall, mannishly tailored, loaded with cameras, met us at the border gate.

"Good to see you lugs."

"Good to see you, Miss Tone," I said.

"Cut the chatter—let's get going."

Turtle said, "We'll take it easy. I'm a sick man."

THE HEEL OF EUROPE

We saw a lot of Spain. Our car went from Rasas to Cape San Sebastián, then to Maturo, to Barcelona—then inland past the Ebro into places as unreal as the craters of the moon, filled with azalea blooms. Miss Tone exposed a lot of film.

The fields of Spain, Turtle said, looked like *malpasso del Infierno*—Hell's back door; calloused scars and giving a feeble crop. A dry period that passed almost unnoticed in the hot hills held the land in a dry fist. Miss Tone became carsick among her camera gear. Fisher held her head and quoted D. H. Lawrence.

The earth dried harder as we went on, until it was mostly massed piled rock, and gray land and yellow land, with now and then the spined ugly Judas trees to keep us company as we went along, not really knowing where we were going. Turtle had quieted down after a period of restlessness. We tanned quickly, not to a seaside tan, but to those brown-leather tans that sun and no water in the air give one. We grew to like the hot facetious winds and even the Zopilote buzzards overhead.

The car went on, and we sat, our tan faces staring ahead, our eyes narrowed to slits behind our sun glasses, and after a shrewd application to the business of driving we were in the high parts. The roads were good for some time, then they got worse, and later on Miss Tone refused to use the local inns' bathrooms. She used to get up early and bathe out of two tins of water some place by the roadside, while we men went for a walk and tried to catch small black lizards with red thread tongues. Then the sun would go high with swollen, ultimate anguish. We ate *garbanzos* (chick peas), drank sour wine, learned to curse (*Santísima María*), learned to curse this land like the farmers did.

It was at this time when Turtle, his nerves cured, could

AMONG THE WEDDING GUESTS

not turn to anything else, that he turned to nature. He had been reading late the night before—something he could not wholly agree with. "That life moves eternally from growth to decline, from decline to dissolution, and from dissolution to new growth."

"This is unfair, old boy. It fills me with pity, and to me pity is more promiscuous than lust."

"That's no mood to cover the Duke of A——'s daughter's wedding," said Miss Tone. "I hope the light is good and they let us right up close."

WEDDING OF A DUKE'S DAUGHTER

We got to Seville and Miss Tone went ahead to the hotel to bathe and was waiting for us in the lobby when we got there.

"You guys are late. I've been cooling my feet here three hours."

"Plenty of time for the wedding."

"I don't like the cloud formations. This empty sky plays hell with the reflected lights."

"The Duke," said Turtle, "is going ahead with the wedding anyway. I'm hungry."

Miss Tone brightened up. "The grub isn't bad in this jernt."

"Good."

They served us a fine *sesos de ternera sevillana* for lunch and a good white wine. They added a few *chicharrones* (pork meat patties), *salchichón* (sausage) with *agua de azahar* (orange blossom punch). The meals are still good in Spain for a special few.

The hotel manager came in to say our car was ready. The marriage procession was just leaving the Duke's five-hundred-year-old palace and heading for church.

"Will there be trouble?" asked Miss Tone hopefully.

The manager shook his head. "Half the population is in jail for today."

"What did they do?"

"Nothing. We are just short of enough police to watch everybody."

"They think of everything," said Fisher.

The cathedral city of Seville is depressing. There is no doubt about that; the people of Spain, the man in the street, in the mill, in the shop, and in the field is caught in a huge rat trap. And Franco and Roman diplomats bait the trap and exploit it.

An old monk Turtle found and admired very much explained it to us. "We eat each other, and they eat us. It is very sad. Spain was a proud land once but now in the hot little mind of the soldier Franco and in the black robes of the Italians our destiny is warped and ruined."

"The town looks gay," Miss Tone said.

"It's the big vulture's big day; the Duke is breeding for posterity."

"I know, we are here to cover the wedding."

The monk grinned. "May we cover it all soon with a shovel."

I could see Spain was tired and hungry. But in the streets Miss Tone shot her camera into the faces of the very fancy people going to the wedding.

There were pictures of the bride all over the pages of the leashed press. María del Fitz-James (*sic!*) y de S——, the Duchess of ——. She had several dozen other titles, but Fisher said there was a paper shortage in Spain. The bridegroom, he went on, looked like something found in a second-class clothing shop; beautifully tinted and dressed. Don Luis de —— y ——, Miss Tone said, "was being bought for stud . . . but I think the line is worked out."

Fisher got some great street shots.

Miss Tone loaded a fresh camera. "The wedding is costing three hundred grand. That's a lot of dough for a country as hungry as Spain."

Turtle nodded. "Three thousand people are invited. But there will be fireworks for all the people who can't fill a spoon."

The wedding was performed by the Archbishop of Valencia, on the steps of the cathedral. It went very well even if someone tried to pick Turtle's pockets. The magnificent altar, in the past reserved only for royalty, was used; as kings were a dime a dozen and the Duke of A—— had forty-nine titles. The royal Ex-Crown Prince of Italy was there. I didn't see him. Miss Tone said, "he was pacing back and forth under a table, worrying that no one would salute him properly." Also present were the Infante of Orleans, the Infante of Bavaria, and the Infante of Bourbon. I must say they sat there stiffly, with ill grace, as if suggesting they had been hired to attend a butcher's wedding and were earning their fees to give the picnic class. The Duke did give a hundred thousand *pesetas* to the cathedral but Turtle doubted if they got a cut of that.

The Duke himself, looking like a smoked herring in a red jacket, stood by looking down at the floor. According to the press he has had a fine past; he descends from a romance. Arabella Churchill, sister of the Duke of Marlborough, fell in love with James Stuart, later James II of England. Her illegitimate son became the Duke of Berwick, a marshal of France, and the man who helped Philip V on the throne of Spain. One of the present Duke's predecessors in the title inspired such a mad passion in the Empress Eugénie before her marriage to Napoleon III that she tried to poison herself. The Berwick and A—— lines merged, making the present Duke a distant cousin of Winston Churchill.

The enemies of the Dukes of A—— seldom fare well. In the sixteenth century the third Duke, asked on his deathbed if he had forgiven his enemies, said, "I have no enemies; I have hanged them all." The present Duke merely lets them starve to death, Fisher said. Fisher was coming to life. I felt there was hope for him.

THE BIG PARTY

The wedding reception was in the Duke's old palace, which in a careless moment had been built in one of Seville's worst slums. There is no reason for this unless the Duke's forefathers were looking for bargains in real estate.

We marched in between police, armed soldiers, and the pushing, thrusting poor, who cheered, wept, howled, and danced in the streets, trying to borrow a little of the glow of the event for their own miserable lives. The guests came in with dignity, and on foot, through the great gates. The gents in tails-and-toppers, the women in mantillas on high combs.

Turtle found the old brandy and soothed his stomach with it, and Miss Tone and myself looked over the seating arrangements. Fisher worked the camera. Only the best of the best nobility sat at the bridal table. There were three tables. Second-string bluebloods sat a little below the salt, and the remaining guests had a third table with just a little less silverware on it. There were twenty chefs in the low kitchen cellars of the palace, working like mad on thousands of pounds of foie gras, beef, ham, and caviar. There were over a hundred waiters and bartenders who rushed drinks to the panting aristocrats after their hot hours in the parching Seville sun.

A little skipping waiter passed with a tray of wine glasses and we stopped him.

"Great day," said Turtle in his tattered Spanish..

THE SOUP OF CHARITY—SPAIN

"Oh, very great!" said the tired little waiter.

"What's cooking?"

The little waiter smiled and put down his tray. "Fifteen hundred pounds of lobsters alone, seven hundred chickens and turkeys, and fifty pounds of goose liver foie gras."

"You like numbers?" asked Miss Tone, taking his picture.

"Before the trouble, when I had the vote, I was a book-keeper in a cinema palace, but the palace is closed now. How is Clara Bow these days?"

"Fine," said Miss Tone. "What else is on the stove?"

"Fifteen hundred pounds of beef and pork. And the drinks! Fourteen thousand, seven hundred twenty-five bottles, the big size, of wine, whisky, sherry, and cognac, to say nothing of anisette, red and white wine, and the best champagne."

"The cognac looks very good," said Turtle, sniffing.

The little waiter looked shy, and picked up his empty tray. "Don't drink it. We are all secret members of the waiters' union here. We drooled a little in the cognac. And also, we . . ."

He went away quickly, and the wedding party grew very wild. The huge wedding cake decorated with sugar roses came in. It had taken a month to build, and the groom and bride cut it with an old sword that was supposed to have been used to drive the last Moor out of Spain. The A——s are full of traditions.

The best people fought for bits of the cake and a *de Santenas* and *de Anrias*, and *de Almodóvar, del Ríos, de Hijares, del Gades;* all got a little trampled and crushed in the rush.

A trio of mules with clipped tails and tasseled heads stood in the courtyard, harnessed to an old Andalusian bridal carriage, and they seemed very uninterested in the whole thing. As we left, Miss Tone fed them some of the wedding cake, but they didn't get excited.

Miss Tone patted the off mule and said, "You can't get a mule excited about marriage. He is not interested in replenishing the earth."

"The married couple," Turtle said, "are going to Hollywood for their honeymoon to be entertained by the Dukes de Wald and del Zanuck . . ."

14 l'amour and Miss Tone

WE ALL went back to Paris, and then Turtle and Fisher flew on to England. Turtle said I was to go to Italy to see if there was any stuff in Rome worth shooting, and Fisher would join me there when I said the word. I was tired in Paris and just sat around looking at the movie script, wondering what-the-hell. And also thinking, Italy is very fancy now and I shall not like it any more.

Miss Tone called and came over. She looked very excited, her skin flushed, her big hands closed tight, and I looked at her and grinned. *"L'amour?"*

"Could be chum, could be."

129

"This time for keeps?"

"Who wants a lease on it? Listen, I need your help with this lug."

"Drops in his wine or quotes from the best poets?"

"Look, you're going to Italy and he's an Italian-American, and he's nuts about what he calls the Old Country . . . where his folks come from."

"Sure, they always come back to see the old family castle."

"It's not just like that with Marco. Come and have lunch with us and meet him."

"I'm only going to Italy to look for film backgrounds."

"Be a pal. I'll hold your hand some time when you need it." Miss Tone was always direct and I saw her point.

"Got it bad?"

"Good or bad, I got it."

"I'm meeting an old artist friend this morning—see you at lunch."

AN ARTIST'S WORLD

France is another country that won a war and didn't do so well with the peace. Everything is beginning to fall apart. The man in the street knows the facts and figures and shakes his head and goes on walking to save the *métro* fare.

The American artist, married to a French woman, told me, "Political and economic catastrophe is close at hand. Inflation has hit hard. It's hard to believe how cheaply we lived here as art students twenty years ago. Those prices are gone for good. Figures and facts are my hobby. Bread costs have jumped forty per cent in the last years and they eat a lot of that good long loaf here. Light and heat have jumped fifteen per cent . . . so it's dark and cold in most flats until company comes. Meat, milk, and tobacco are luxuries now to lots of Frenchmen."

"Everybody looks busy," I said.

"Trade is down. There is a six-hundred-million-dollar trade deficit, and we owe four hundred million to the European Union. The war in Indo-China is cursed in the streets —it costs a billion francs a day. A hundred million dollars a year is poured into special-works jobs, a kind of boondoggling for votes. Taxes are on food and goods mostly, so the well-endowed evade personal income taxes. Industry is worn out, the machines are junk in many plants. For three years the U.S.A. pumped in two and a half billion dollars, but the country is still pale, no red blood. It's a nation of fat and bankrupt virtues, a hesitant and a moaning population that likes good food, plenty of wine, and a something buried besides the old dog under the fireplace, for a rainy day and hard times."

"They look all right."

"Napoleon killed off the bright young men—the three German invasions killed off more. What is left are mostly the warped, the cunning, the greedy, and the special groups of bank, church, factory, labor union, Royalists, Fascists, Reds, and just plain crackpots. And a very lovely nation and some fine cities and much art."

"I guess you're not coming back," I said.

"This is my home."

"How's painting these days?" I asked.

"Hard—so many new ideas, so many good things of the past tossed away."

"Getting anything good?"

"Suddenly fragments of it will explain themselves for me, beg me to understand, roll at my feet like puppies. But, not often . . ."

"Like how?" I asked.

"Like puppies . . . little riddles of the universe damping your floor as they bark out their small secrets, and some section of your design will then have a true sort of unity. The more I see of art, the more I am aware of its frailty, its shifting, dissolving, changing. These unresolved discords to the artist are the captured vision, experiences made only to him, and to those of us who hang his work."

He stopped talking and looked down at his hands. I noticed his eyes were focused. This was a lonely man, perhaps even a great man. When he spoke again, he spoke low, without bombast.

"Art is not a shore lit by lighthouses—art is more like a mist—an enveloping wonder and awe in which we exist from consciousness to the final darkness. To define this atmosphere of mind and marrow, and leave out a lot of the alien and external, is a life's work. To trace a succession of images, thoughts, and impressions is art. To create a glowing mist that mirrors the surface of consciousness. A great job."

"Sure," I agreed.

"The best art is individualistic, protestant, nonconformist —a personal sense of discovery of man and nature. Suspect authority, tradition, and convention in science, religion, and social phrases. Find life bit by bit, and turn your back to public opinion. Only in extreme circumstances does the human spirit rise to any stature."

He frowned again. He knew he had exposed himself and his secrets and he didn't like it.

"Let me put it this way. The true artist never liked what the mob liked. And so in art some got tired of landscapes fried in onion and bacon grease to get that patina. That's all right for meatheads like J. P. Morgan or Frick or Kress or Mellon. They're real ignorant of anything that Lord Duveen didn't fake and pin onto their drawers like a kid with a sign on him in school, written by his mother—*I unbutton here.*"

"Thanks. What does it add up to?" I asked.

"I don't say I'm a great artist. I teach a lot of nonsense

about form and line, you understand an artist *must* know these things, the eternal shapes, and then how to change them. But I'll tell you a secret, the artist, the modern artist is failing because he forgets he is also the historian of society, not just of abstract dreams. And that's the rub, how to remain an artist and a human being at the same time. Painting machines? Hell, I can show you a dozen great ones. Inventors of forms and schools? I used to have a new one to amaze the world every month. But being able to paint like an angel and invent like an angel is nothing but empty victory unless it means something to the artist in his brief journey between two sleeps, as Shakespeare says."

"I see."

"It's all right to paint bottles and apples and the muscles of violins and fruit bowls, but you can't put down all humanity and philosophy in a rosebud, or a new way of understanding in a seashell. The study of man, as another damn Englishman said, *is* man."

I said I was trying to do just that . . .

THE MAN FROM AMERICA

I went to an Italian café on the rue Boissonade and I met Marco, Miss Tone's friend. He was a large, round man with heavy arms and a blue-black face that looked as if he shaved it with sandpaper every two hours; there was always just a tiny smear of shaving lather under one large red ear. He looked as if he were a self-made man and rather proud of the job. Miss Tone introduced me.

"Hello, fella," he said when we sat down. "This place is good?"

Miss Tone said, "The best Italian place in France."

"What's cooking?" asked Marco.

"*Buon giorno,*" said the waiter.

Marco ignored him. I saw he didn't know Italian.

"That means good morning," I said.

"It does?"

I said to the waiter, "*Sogliole alla marinara* . . . for three."

"Thanks, fella."

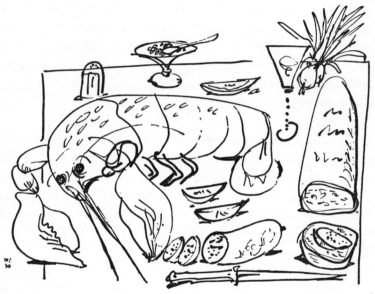

ITALIAN CAFÉ

Even Marco admitted that it was fine food as he finished on sausage and *finocchio* seeds and *pizzefritte* cake. He ate with a sad hunger that seemed to say, I don't want food, but what else can I get? Miss Tone smiled at him sadly.

"*E nostro piacere,*" the waiter said.

After lunch, Marco handed me a good cigar and opened the first two buttons on his vest and drank a lemon in hot water ("for my gut, buddy," he said), and then he said, "So it's a deal, fella? You'll show us Italy?"

"Well," I said, "I don't know if I know Italy as well as that. You are the Banana King of Long Island?"

"Sweet potato," said Marco with his first smile. "I hate the damn bananas. I guess you can't buy a sweet yam north of the Mason-Dixon Line without Marco K. Pagano getting his cut."

"Listen," said Miss Tone, "my chum, Stevie, he knows Italy—right down to the last little naked pickineeno."

Marco nodded, and I noticed a tick in his cheek. "Always I say fella, to myself, you are the big shot. Why not go home and see the Old Country before they bump you off?"

"Bump you off?" I asked.

"Don't worry," said Marco, "only back on Long Island. Some guys don't like the way I peddle my yams."

Miss Tone grinned, "Exciting, isn't it?"

"The Old Country," I said. "I wish I were home myself."

"I'm sad," said Marco.

"Very well," said Miss Tone. "You *are* sad . . . me am only thinking me am sad."

So we drank to everybody's Old Country and Marco began to cry because we were right guys, see, and not two-timing scuts, see . . .

HUNT FOR THE OLD COUNTRY

And much later we got on the *wagon-lit* and I fell asleep and slept a long time and when I got up and looked out my window I was in Italy.

"This *can't* be Italy," Marco said to the ornate train guard with the bad teeth.

"*Ma quando chiacchiera,*" he said, "but it is!"

"Oh, no."

"*Madonna mia,* I should know. I am Italian."

So Marco accepted it and we went in to breakfast and Marco ate rice in *conserva di pomidori* and I explained to the waiter that while he was not *nato'n America* . . . *Per l'amore di Dio* . . . not to think he was a lousy native. He lived on

Long Island and see, no back talk! Marco was not happy. He looked confused, as if somehow he had come on a fool's errand and hated to admit it.

"*Ma, sì, sì,*" said the waiter.

"Now let's see the Old Country," said Marco to me and Miss Tone.

We saw Italy. Beginning with the Piedmontese Alps. We went westward from Gressoney-St.-Jean to Chatillon, then beyond Brusson to Codigoro. Marco looked sad and wrinkled his face and said, "No dice."

"Honey," said Miss Tone, "it's going to be all right."

We asked for the Old Country. They shrugged their shoulders. Our guides swore.

We went south to Bassa Italia. We got into trouble by asking for clean bath water. We wanted plumbing that worked. Miss Tone refused to let the waiter scratch himself. We were called *ruffiani. Per Bacco.* We went on and I saw much beauty and talked to the *paesani* and asked about a place Marco could have come from. But his memory was dim, all the people he had once known were dead. Every place he said they lived like pigs; his people, the guides agreed, lived *non come porchi.* I think he really knew nothing much of his past. Somehow he had expected to find it easy.

We went from place to place. I ran out of toothbrushes, and a cook at an inn ate my toothpaste but said it would *never* replace salad dressing. Marco grew careless of shaving. Sometimes he didn't speak for hours.

ROME IN DECLINE

We went to Rome on a hot, chrome-yellow day.

"This is Rome?" said Marco one day in our hotel suite.

"All of it outside the window," Miss Tone said.

"But this is not the Old Country."

THE POOR STEAL

I agreed and went for a walk.

Italy is an unhappy place. It is not all the tourists' Palazzo
Venezia or the Borghese Gardens or drinking *Capri bianca*.
The land is worn out, a museum of Roman remains and goat
dung. The big landlords still own most of it, and the well-to-do
and the rich manage to avoid paying most of their income
taxes. The Reds know this and make big fun of it and win converts, and the leaders of the nation look the other way, for
paying taxes is something the well-to-do think is a lousy
American habit.

Everyone steals. The government steals, the poor steal, the
rich steal. The poor steal bread and rags, and the rich Italians
steal American supplies—Marshall Plan aid. The Reds steal,

the Catholic Action kids steal, and everyone shrugs it off with "living is hard."

On the Via Imperiale they drink and salute each other "*A Noi*," and the best-organized black market in Europe is cheerfully accepted. "A hot Picasso? A ton of coal? A technicolor print of *Gone with the Wind? Fortunatissimo*, are you the man who is looking for a drawing by Titian? *Sì, eccellenza*, a carload of Bel Paese cheese has come on the market. *Ming*, how cheap it's going to the damn Greeks. *Mangi et taci!*"

The Church is deeply involved in politics, trade, and land holdings. *Pax Romana* is wormy with hunger and age, and only among a few artists are new things being done. The beggars are back, the trains no longer run on time, the dirty hard times of the *Fasci di Combattimento* have few followers, but these very powerful. It's an old story for the Italians. They are, in the main, a people who can on the surface make love and sing and eat the *pasta*, but under this is a deep, cruel hardness polished by misery for a long time, tired of ritual and manifesto and big words and ideals and heavens on paper. Only to stay alive is enough . . .

LIVING IN THE PAST

We stayed a week and we got rooms in a fair neighborhood among the housing that clusters thickly behind the Piazza di Spagna, and we wandered over the staircases and hills and found at last the peeling yellow house of the Giacomettis. They lived in a big flat—five floors up—smelling of olive oil and goat cheese and babies and holy candles. Cesare Guido Giacometti was a balloon-shaped man past middle age who had lived in Chicago at one time and read racing forms and detective stories.

He shook our hands. "What the hell! Glad to see an American again."

BIANCA AND BABY

"Glad enough to rent them rooms?" Miss Tone asked.

"Bianca!" shouted the master of the house, scratching himself in the belly and smiling.

Bianca was suckling a dark naked baby, and two others just beginning to walk hung to her skirts and ate their fingers, their beautiful eyes on the strangers.

"My friends from America . . . they wanta rooms."

"Oh, America," she said, shifting the feeding baby to the other breast, where it ate and grunted, the soft top of its head pulsing with the effort.

Guido asked, "You Coca-Cola salesmen?"

"No."

"Good, you can stay here."

After a while Marco got restless again. He was hungry for something besides the cigar he was chewing. "I came to find a place. There are too many places here. It's not big like Texas, but big enough."

"It's Italy." I said, writing out a wire to Fisher to join me in a week.

"It's only Rome, see, and it's not what I come for. Get it?"

"How about Capri?" Miss Tone asked.

"What do they do there?"

"See the Blue Grotto."

"To hell with dives. What else?"

"Sit on the sand . . . talk to the girls," I said.

"I didn't come here for broads. Pardon me, baby. Look, fella, I been a long time thinking of coming home to the Old Country. I gotta feel like I felt when I was a kind of a small kid. A bare-assed kid and flies all around maybe—but a kid. This Rome ain't it. It's only Newark, New Jersey, only more sidewalks."

I could see he was homesick for something out of his past . . . for something he had come a long way to find and now it was lost or we hadn't found it, and he was beginning to wonder what was the matter. And he was angry at us and getting madder.

"Where did your folks come from?" I asked.

"Italy! And don't say *this* is it!"

"What part?" Miss Tone asked.

"Part? I was a small-fry kid with no shirt on. It was hot. There was sun. And grapes. I remember the old man plowing big fields and my mother tending grapevines on a hill. And the smoking olive oil in the pan, and the goats all over everything. Boy, it was all wonderful in some daffy way . . . and pretty, I guess, like a punch in the nose. I can see it all. Show it to me!"

"Well . . ." I said.

"What's the matter? You think a guy is a sissy because he thinks something is pretty?"

"No, Marco, only didn't all this beauty have a name?"

"Sure, but I never went to school in those days. I was only a very dumb kid . . . so no cracks about my memory." He looked at me with very large black eyes and I saw this thing was making him sick.

"Did it snow? Was there wind? Were there green trees ever in blossom?" Miss Tone asked.

"What's this song title you're handing me? Look, I'm the sweet potato big shot of Long Island and if I thought you was pulling a rib . . ."

I got out a timetable. "Can the chatter, Marco [I had learned how to talk that way from the Paris cinemas]. We'll go look for the Old Country in the south."

"I've been to Miami Beach."

"The toe of the boot of Italy. Your Old Country sounds like the vineyards down there. What color were the goats?"

"The goats? Black and white with red eyes."

"The south sounds like it." I tried to sound very sure.

Marco sat down and fanned himself with his Panama hat. ("They weave *this* underwater; how they hold their breaths, I don't know.") He threw away his cigar sadly. "A guy does what he thinks is right . . . never forgets his old lady's grave . . . buries his brother-in-laws . . . and then when he wants to see the Old Country, they pull it away from under him. It ain't fair. I been looking forward to this for a long, long time. I ain't running away from nothing. Well, not much. You understand anything I'm saying?"

"I understand, Marco," said Miss Tone tenderly. "We'll find the Old Country."

"I know I sound like a patsy— soft in the noggin—but I guess when you want to see the Old Country, well, you want to see the Old Country. And that's all there is to it!"

"How has the food been?" I asked.

"I et better at the Oyster Bar in Grand Central. Everything cooked in erl . . . and I'm tired of miles of *pasta*. Jeez, these wops is killing themselves in erl."

DO YOU REMEMBER SCOTTY?

There was a little Armenian place in Rome where my Uncle Willie used to go with F. Scott Fitzgerald, in the days when they went to places like that, and I decided to go there and see if their famous Armenian salad called *Haigaga Aghtzan*, was still served. It was, and they were just mixing a huge wooden bowl of it.

My Uncle Willie brought the recipe back to America and it's very good the way he used to make it, but of course he didn't have the fat arms of the salad mixer in Rome, who flirted with us while she mixed the salad, and dished it out with a wooden shovel of scented cedar wood.

We had our salad with a fruit compote and some Greek wine but I could see Marco was not happy at any of this. After the wine he began to weep and say that he was an unhappy man. And the owner of the place came over and rolled her big black eyes and said *che brutta fortuna* and I said he was lonely for home, and she said *è vero* and offered to take us to a native wedding but Marco said we had to go south at dawn. This was bad because Marco was a bull of a man who either ate a thing, broke it, or slept with it. He didn't admit there was anything else you could do with anything.

ITALIAN KIDS

15   south in the boot

THE village of Kanza is not on any map I ever saw. It clings to a rocky mountainside. The clutter of clay and stone shapes that are houses look like bee nests plastered onto the cliffs with mud. There is only one street and it is paved with rocks and the oxen seem to have one side of them shorter than the other so that their two short legs (on one side) keep them walking level.

Our hired car panted to a stop, gave out an Italian sigh, blew steam, and died. The driver, who had once been a boot-black in Frisco ("sonamagun, thata one fine place"), looked at us and then up at the cliff dwellings.

143

"This as far as Henry Ford he wanta go."

"That the village of Kanza?" Miss Tone asked.

"If she no Kanza, we one damn fools to coma this far."

Marco looked up at the village and said, "What's the idea of this cheap hangout?"

"It's Kanza. There are several old families here named Pagano. I think it's the Old Country."

Marco grew suddenly silent and he looked around him with awe and then sniffed and we started to climb slowly. It was a hard trek but we made it and stood by a shaggy stone hut overgrown with wild hay on its roof. An old man sat at the curb milking a goat.

I explained I was looking for a Pagano. He said there is no such name. All the Paganos came from the north of Italy and were of noble families.

"What are they called here?" Miss Tone asked.

"Paganos. We accent the o . . . you accented the p."

"I'm sorry," I said. "Do you remember any Pagano who went to America, maybe about thirty, forty years ago?"

The goat looked at me with wonder. It may have been my new tie (a gift from Marco). The old man closed his eyes to think. The sun was very yellow on the old stones. Then the old man opened his eyes. "Yes, they went away to America and became very rich. There was a story in a paper my daughter read to me once (I am not a student, you understand, just a goat herder). She said our relatives . . . we are third cousins . . . she said they had struck it rich and changed their name to Rockefeller."

"It said that in the paper?" Miss Tone asked.

"So my daughter said. She can't read well but there was a picture of my second cousin Pagano in the paper and he *was* called Rockefeller, she read."

Marco hadn't moved or said anything. He was looking at a

GROUP IN VILLAGE CHURCH

stone hut, the third one on the cliff. "Say, I think I remember this place. It's the third hut down."

I said to the old man, "Where did your second cousin live?"

"Oh," said the old man, pushing the goat away (but she stayed like an old lean woman listening to gossip). "The hut is no longer standing. This village is new. We had to pull it down. 'Big Chin,' long ago, he said it was not modern. So we pulled it down . . . every hut. And then we rebuilt it. All the huts from the old stones but we mixed up the places where they stood. I do not understand this modern progress."

Marco had walked a little apart and now he came back, his cigar unlit in his scowling face, and said gruffly to Miss Tone, "Come on, baby, let's get outa here, see . . . I wanta go. Come on."

THE LOST COUNTRY

That night at the hotel, Marco packed his bag and shook his head. "It's no dice, fella. This ain't the Old Country. Not to me, anyway. I guess you gotta stay and grow up with it or it ain't the Old Country at all. I lost it some place. I don't know where. But we're not going to find it any more."

I could see he was puzzled and shocked and I felt sorry for him, because in my own way I was looking for the Old Country of Art, and I was finding it a little bit here, and a little bit there, but for Marco . . . well, it was not going to be that way. Miss Tone held his hand tight.

"You see, fellas, I guess I had my Old Country. It's called Long Island. Ever been there? Well, it's a lot of places to lots of guys. Me, I was up to my navel in sweet potatoes all my life and dreaming of the Old Country, and I guess I was in it all the time, see, and never caught wise."

"I see, Marco," Miss Tone said.

"So, I'm going home. I'm catching the next boat out of Naples and if you was smart, you mugs, you'd go home, too. What have these ginzos got for us? You'll only sperl your life here among these guys. *Our* Old Country is over there! You're American, too, ain't you?"

And he gave me some cigars and he went away in the hired car for Naples and Miss Tone cried a little. She said sadly, later as we had a few drinks, "I knew it wouldn't work, but I gave it a spin. Now I want to think Marco lived happy and contented on Long Island and built himself a Cape Cod house and collected Early American furniture and joined the Book-of-the-Month Club. A solid citizen of the Old Country out there someplace beyond the polo fields of Meadowbrook, no longer hunting something, no longer sweating in the night."

Miss Tone flew back to Paris and Fisher came to Rome with

the camera. We did a lot of shots of streets and buildings and the gardens and fountains of Rome.

ORDERS TO THE EAST

When we got back to London, Fisher found his orders to report to the Army, and most likely to ship out to Malaya—

DUTY IN MALAYA

which he didn't like or care for. He left scowling with two weeks' extra pay. I never did understand him. A bitter young man, a mixed-up young man, and the joy of life wasn't in him. Perhaps there is no reason why it should have been. There was a little more elbow room around when I was a young man. A little more sun in the sky.

At the studio we ran off all the film we had shot and Mac came over from Paris and he helped us look at it.

I said, "Let's give it up. It's no good."

"It's beautiful color," said Mac.

"It's exciting footage," said Turtle, holding his stomach.

I said, "But it's not a picture, it's just a lot of stock shots. You need stars and a director and a film editor."

Mac nodded. "I've been busy. I've hired a producer from Hollywood to help Turtle. He's —— ——. Ever hear of him?"

I nodded. "Chicken Fat we used to call him. But what about a cameraman now that Fisher is gone?"

"I've got a director and cameraman. Ever hear of Mike Murd?"

"In the old days . . . I don't remember clearly," I said.

"He's joining you in Hong Kong," Mac said, expressionless.

"Who, me?" I asked, stupidly.

"Yes, I've decided to go the whole hog on this picture. I want real stuff in Asia, India, Africa. I don't care what it costs. But get real stuff."

I didn't say anything more just then, because when you are in the motion picture business, you don't expect anything to sound real, and the craziest things happen that you know can't happen, but they do. Besides, they had a contract with me, and they were paying me. And I had seen a lot worse ideas turn into money-making films. I don't know why and I can't explain it, but these things happen this way in the picture business, and when you repeat them to outsiders, they sound like a poor-grade dream.

I remember running into D. W. Griffith one day in a small bar on Sunset Boulevard in Los Angeles, and him saying, "The reason no one can't write well about Hollywood is that no matter how truly you write it down, it sounds like fantasy. The real things that happen to you here make people rub their eyes and say, 'No, it couldn't be.' "

So in the end I repacked, took some more medical shots, and got on some other planes, with a script that had been so changed and marked up that it looked like something Einstein had been working on for years.

ASIA ON THE HORIZON

The story line was no clearer when the plane circled over the harbor of the island of Hong Kong, and I saw below the streets and the buildings on the hills over the harbor and the British flag (one of the passengers on the plane said, "The sun never sets on the damn rag because God doesn't trust it in the dark").

There were more soldiers, and more rich-looking people, and more poor-looking people; otherwise, Hong Kong looked

THE POOR OF HONG KONG

just like the travel films back home. The smell wasn't like buttered popcorn either.

On the way out I had read in the volume of Lawrence that Turtle had given me as a parting gift:

> I doubt if there is even one of us who has ever known so much as an apple, a whole apple. All we know is shadows, even of apples. Shadows of everything, of the whole world, shadows even of ourselves. We are inside the tomb, and the tomb is wide and shadowy like hell, even if sky-blue by optimistic paint, so we think it is all the world. But our world is a wide tomb full of ghosts, replicas. We are all spectres, and we have not been able to touch even so much as an apple. Spectres we are to one another. Spectre you are to me, spectre I am to you. Shadow you are even to yourself. And by shadow I mean idea, concept, the abstracted reality, the ego. We are not solid. We don't live in the flesh. Our instincts and intuitions are dead, we live wound round with the winding sheet of abstraction.

book 3

IN OTHER PLACES OTHER FACES

HONG KONG—ANTIAIRCRAFT GUNS

16   Hong Kong blues

ASIA, tormented to ferment, is a lost world in many ways. Malaya is full of armed people in hot jungles who fight each other, each side calling the other bandits. In Burma there is much trouble and the English in the best clubs talk about it and shake their heads. It's all over, the days of Kipling soldiers, tin and rubber fortunes in the old sense. In Iran the fanatics shout and the oil bubbles. In Indo-China former Nazi storm troopers, Polish officers, and French farmboys fight in a French Army just hanging on by its teeth and a little Marshall help. The horizons are all on fire . . .

All of this one can hear from eyewitnesses in Hong Kong, this island rock where the old firms that remember their opium war days still are in business. Jardine, Matheson and Company, and many others. But their days are numbered and they know it. The registered tonnage in the harbor is screened and guarded, but much of it gets away somehow with its cargoes to the coast of Red China. Across the way is the staring face of the China shoreline glaring back at Hong Kong, and one can feel the hate and heat that will one day sweep away the last outpost of white men on the China Sea.

Life goes on at Hong Kong as if nothing in a social sense has changed. Three hundred and ninety-one square miles of ten thousand Britons, two million Chinese. The tea parties are bigger, the fashion show finer, the polo ponies battle each other over the sea-rock hedges of fields carrying Eton- and Oxford-bred meat on their backs. Civil servants and their ladies (and their mistresses) and their suntanned children stand in formal gardens. The Number One and Two and Three Boys walk softly and serve them, but they no longer keep their eyes lowered with respect.

The banks look strong as ever. The Hong Kong and Shanghai Bank is old guard, old school tie, staffed by Noel Coward-looking men with sleek hair and pale eyes, who wilt into their clean white shirts. But the new Bank of China (owned and run by Communists) does big business, and mocks the old days of a safe forty-per-cent profits per year when the Old China Hands had things their own way and enjoyed floggings and half-breed children.

No one will talk openly about the fate of this island. No one will talk about it at polite dinners, over gin slings in the good bars, at the tennis matches where proper young people play a good backhand and sweat neatly into their thin white clothes, starched clean every morning.

But there are places where the clerks and the half-breeds live, where the sweepers and the Number One Boys have their families, and there one senses and hears a lot about the time

WHERE THE HALF-BREEDS LIVE

when all this will be swept away. The police walk sternly, and
the coolies grin and spit on the sidewalk after they pass. There
is no real peace of mind, no feeling tomorrow will be cooler,
better, safer.

SUSPENSE AND HEAT

The native waiter at my elbow hands me the damp newspaper—the English-speaking one—and sets the silver coffee
pot just right and stands back. His back is not bent over as far
as it used to be, I'm sure, and he looks ironically amused when
you suspect the eggs. And when the coffee is gritty, he shrugs

a little and slowly takes the pot back to the kitchen. He's in no hurry, not the way he used to be. And you feel, what are you doing here? What is going to happen here? And you are thankful you don't have to live here and keep face and give tea parties and raise up long-toothed children and try and get respect from a people who hate you.

Hong Kong is fifty years out of date. It exists in a pool of stale history, smelling of money and white women dying slowly in the tropics. In the harbor the ships load and unload, and everyone is making a fortune (or hoping to) in misery, blood, and revolts.

MIKE MURD

I sat in the hotel room talking to the big wide man, the new cameraman and director.

"It's a hassel making a picture this way," he said.

Tired gray smoke came up from the faded colors of the Chinese part of Hong Kong.

Mike Murd (that's close enough to his name) had been a great director back in the days when pictures didn't talk; but voice, three wives, and a habit of collecting scotch in full bottles had seen him turned into a very fine second-unit manager.

"I know," I said.

Mike, his red face redder, his red hair thin, and his smile a little droopy, looked down on the island city.

"What are we here for?" he asked. "Really?"

"Background shots for Chicken Fat's new epic."

Chicken Fat was our new Hollywood producer, a great big lug with two behinds and a legend that he sweated chicken fat when excited, and he was always excited. He directed us by cable from Hollywood and Turtle did the same from London.

"Funny-looking place," said Mike.

"That daffy temple is the Court of Vigorous Fertility."

"You're talking to a man with three wives . . . stop kidding."

"It's a great town, I hear, if you have money and don't care too much."

"I don't care as long as Chicken Fat can't reach us."

"They have a good cable office here."

CHINESE HONG KONG

We went out to see the town. A broken-down flivver took us along the *hutungs* or native lanes to a peeling hotel . . . a place that had real Western chairs. We decided to move in here to get real local color.

Mike found the bar and asked for a drink. The Chinese bar boy, a man of fifty, nodded, and asked, "Yes, sir. What?"

Mike turned to me. "What's a slug of bourbon called here?"

"They distill from rice and corn here." I said to the bar boy, "Any *Pai-kan*?"

"Rumor has it it's made from millet and dove droppings," Mike said. "We'll try it."

"It's got sixteen mule legs in it, Mike."

"I'll try it . . . you, too."

So we had a bowl each—those little China bowls of *Kao Liang,* and Mike drank and I drank, and Mike winked and took a prizefighter pose and said, "Sissy stuff. Why it ain't even dropped past my gall bladder."

The bar man and I smiled. "Don't worry, Mike, you'll get it past your toes yet."

"Give us a bottle and we'll have lunch. What's good here, ole boy . . . black eggs and pickled grandmothers?"

I ordered a lobster-garlic dinner with turnip Shantung, and bean curd rind. And with a bottle of *Kao Liang* we sat down to dinner. The waiter handed me a cable, but Mike took it from my hand.

"It's from Chicken Fat, I'm sure. Don't open it. Don't let it spoil our lunch. Gotta lot of drinking to do of this local soda water."

We began with a sort of jello soup made of bird's nest lining. Then there was the famous Peiping Duck, which I passed, but Mike loved. It's made by emptying a duck, stuffing it with spices and hanging it in its feathers in a mild place for six months. It was followed by fried prawns and a soup made from stocks over ten years old. Then the lobster-garlic, which is the king of all dishes in Asia. Bamboo shoots, scalded mutton, and a white tree fungus cooked in wine. This may sound like a lot of food, but there was just a taste of each on a small dish.

The place was well known for other native foods, but I felt I could wait a few days until my stomach went native. Boiled bear's paw, tortoise egg almost raw, fried fish lips, water chestnuts and chicken silk (which is chicken in very smooth cream) and puddings of lotus root and millet.

ORDERS FROM CHICKEN FAT

After dinner I opened the cable:

> CROSS TO RED CHINA NEED CLOSE-UP FIGHTING
> REAL BURNING BUILDING FOR LOVE SCENE PROC-
> ESS SHOTS C.F.

Mike sipped his green Chinese tea and made a sound dismissing Chicken Fat. "Nuts to that. We'll do it in Hong Kong. I'm going to film some singsong girls."

Mike got up and sat down suddenly with a general paralysis. "Say . . . it *must* be the weather."

I watched the waiter carry off the *Kao Liang*.

We didn't get any singsong girl shots that day. The next morning I went down to the press office of a British news service and found a slim blond man throwing cards into a hat placed about ten feet away from him on the floor.

"You're Bleers?" I asked.

"I am."

"They say you know the ropes," I said.

"A bit."

I told him about our plans and he brightened up and put away the cards. "A dingo beano . . . singsong girls, and on the old expense account, I hope?"

I said yes. He shook the cards out of his hat and got into a shabby Burberry coat that had lost most of its Bond Street trim.

"Green Garbo's the spot . . . singers and dancers from Suchow and Kaifeng, Tsinan. And fine food. Real Haig and Haig and *rijstaffel*. I better change my shirt."

"Look, Bleers, we're just going to film some background stuff, not taking any royal suite."

"The royal suite is taken . . . some War Lord from Changsha has desk space there."

THE GREEN GARBO

THE GREEN GARBO

We picked up Mike, feeling a little unsteady, and in an alley behind a red-tiled palace we found an iron-bound door that Bleers seemed to be known at, and we were in a long room heated by charcoal stoves and a record playing an old Noel Coward tune, "Someday I'll Find You." A very tall and beautiful Chinese woman came toward us.

"Dinner and dancing?" she asked.

"And singing," said Mike. "I got a sound unit with me."

"This is the Green Garbo," said Bleers to us. And to the Chinese lady, "These chaps are from Hollywood. Want to take some of the local hanky-panky."

"Metro-Goldwyn-Mayer paid me a thousand dollars a night. That was for *The Good Earth*."

"We're not making anything that big," said Mike. "Look honey, the swindle sheet can stand two hundred bucks. Is it a deal?"

"Food and dancing extra?" asked the Green Garbo.

"It's a deal." Mike held out a ham of a hand.

"I like you. Red hair is lucky."

"Not for me," said Mike. "Shall we set up the camera now?"

"Yes," I said.

She held out a beautiful pale green hand. I placed two hundred dollars in it and wondered how Chicken Fat and Turtle would react to spending money on singing girls. Just then the hotel porter came in with a fresh cable. I didn't even open it. The Green Garbo went to wake up the girls, and Mike went out to see if the power truck had come up. And I sat down and wondered how I was going to work this place into our musical, which now was about a poor Chinese boy (Marlon Brando) who finds that bandits have stolen his girl (Ava Gardner) and sold her to Ronald Colman (or whoever it was that Chicken Fat had under contract) and Ronnie takes her on his yacht (everybody in pictures owns a yacht) and falls in love with her, and finds out, after he married her, that her mother was an English schoolteacher who had married a white Russian prince in Djokjakarta (don't blame me for this part of the story, I was only hired to get the proper Chinese background into this part of Chicken Fat's drug dream; Turtle seemed to have turned it all over to him).

The girls were very neat and two of them could speak U.S. Marine English, having met some of the lads during the war. They were thin and very slim and very modern and had short haircuts and wanted to know who had won the Rose Bowl. They played little stringed things like demented banjos and sang fearful sounds out of thin, pretty lips and let us see their beautiful legs through slits in their costumes. It was all as

proper as a Vassar daisy chain as I explained to Bleers (who
had expected another kind of daisy chain) but I explained
that time was so valuable to movie people we couldn't afford
to have too much fun on the job. But if Mike got all the footage
he wanted, maybe after dinner I would have the girls recite
for him.

"I say, that's fearfully decent of you."

"How is the rioting in Hong Kong?"

"Oh, everyone seems to take a pot shot at everyone else
once in a while."

"Any chance of getting some action stuff?"

"Not a bloody. Just local popping and pecking away from
rooftops. Once in a while a bomb, but fearful bombs . . .
homemade and not very effective . . . just messy!"

The girls sat in a group and sang. Then two of them danced
very close together and did graceful things with their fingers,
and they swayed and put on masks and danced some more. It
would look very good on film. Mike was very pleased, and
kissed the Green Garbo, who looked surprised, and he said,
"Put it on the bill."

Dinner was very fine. We sat on mats and ate from a low
table and Mike took one end of the table and the Green Garbo
took the other end, and the girls really made the chopsticks
fly. We had *bo lo kai* as the main dish, a mixture of chicken
and pineapple and nuts and shoots, with a side dish of *ching
yu*—a bean sauce and garlic version of steamed bass. *Cha
shiu*, roast pork, and Dragon's Eyes noodles.

The meal ended with three bottles of wine . . . *moi cheung*,
sauce flavored with plums, a litchi nut called *lai chee*, and the
usual *hang yan peang*, almond cakes, and very hot green *cha*
(tea).

"You're a great kid," said Mike to the Green Garbo.

"*Ts'ao t'a ma-ti pi*," said the Green Garbo, which was a

neat way of using an oath to mean: you're a damn charming liar.

"You ought to be in pictures."

"Listen, Mike," I said, "no screen tests."

ONE RIOT, COMING UP

At which point I felt we had better leave. I got Bleers into a ricksha and we went back to the hotel trotting along at six *li* an hour (a *li* being about a third of a Chinese mile). At the hotel the owner, a fat gentleman with a smiling face, called Kwong Lung Tai, and his small son-in-law with the

THE HOTEL OF LUNG TAI

English education, Yan Hung-ming Sang, were waiting up for me and each had a cable from Chicken Fat. I felt it was no use opening them.

"Had a fine evening," said Bleers. "Real jolly and you're all such nice chaps."

"You were a great help. Think nothing of it."

"You're all fine chaps . . . even Mike, even if he says we English were always on the wrong side . . . *your* side."

"Mike's Irish, and his idea of the English is not fit for fine company," I said.

"Must show you a new place just opened under the Red Road. Run by an ex-dancer of the court of the last king of Indo-China. Minnie Wen Hai is a close friend of mine, and . . ."

At that moment the hotel porter came in and rushed up to the hotel owner and recited what seemed a long excited poem in Chinese.

Kwong Lung Tai ran his fingers through his little beard and turned to me. "Your friend can get fine picture of a riot at south pier."

"Will it keep till morning?" Mike asked.

"It can be arranged," said the hotel keeper.

"You see, the light is bad now for pictures."

Bleers said, "I suppose if you pay them enough they can hold off till morning."

"Is it that kind of an organized riot?" I asked.

"It's a local affair . . . for control of the rice market in the black dealing."

I had never bought off a riot before. "I'm kinda new at this, Bleers. What do you usually pay to delay riots?"

Bleers said, "Don't give 'em more than ten dollars, American."

Kwong Lung Tai rolled his eyes and his small son-in-law Yan Hung-ming Sang rolled his, and said, "A real riot . . .

two bombs and maybe we can arrange a rotten fruit charge, very striking."

Bleers asked, "Any real beatings?"

"Please, these are men with families . . . maybe a broken leg . . . but that is extra."

I turned to Bleers. "This is all rather confusing. What kind of rioting goes on here?"

"Oh, it's all rather formal political rioting. If one side hurts a man on the other side, inside the city here, then they have to go out and hurt someone on the other side the next time . . . and it cuts into the black-market business."

"Well," I said, "I'm not a bloodthirsty man and it's a rotten movie anyway. Just have the boys mix it up at dawn . . . and no hurting. I'll give ten dollars, American, with a little hitting over the head with bamboos and a good rotten fruit charge."

"Six o'clock?" Mike said.

"Make it eight."

We all bowed and I felt like Churchill or Marshall or a football captain; here I was running a little war all my own. I could see now why generals in power are such a danger. Calling the turns in a battle are bad habits to get into.

I was up at dawn and found Mike pouring ice water over his head and I got him and the camera into a flivver and we started for the south pier. It was a clear gray day, with a mist of weak smoke rising from the houses, and already the ricksha boys tearing around the town and the towers of the banks were like fine art against a blue steel sky. I could smell and feel the life around me beginning another day of toil, turmoil, and trouble, and somehow I felt very sorry for Asia trapped somehow in its destiny. To be always exploited, hungry, and sad. I was in a mood where I felt for every hungry stomach and every aching head and every troubled fam-

HONG KONG RIOT-MAKER

ily in the city. The British and the Greeks and the rest of the Americans still slept.

We went along rutted streets and ended up at a yellow wall, with groups of men in padded cotton sleeping on the cold clay ground.

Mike said, "*This* is the riot?"

The son-in-law nodded, "I get them going."

Mike held his aching head. "Wouldn't trade this head for a million dollars, Chinese."

"Better get your cameras set up."

It was a great riot. The bamboos whacked heads and there was a striking rotten fruit charge, and the stains were wonderful as they cut into a mud courtyard, and we had to pay extra for a valuable umbrella that got torn. The police came and broke it up quickly.

We shipped the film out by plane and went back to the hotel and rested. There was a cable from Chicken Fat written in his best third-grade English:

> RESHOOTING NIGHT CLUB STUFF IN STUDIO
> YOUR FOOTAGE LOOKS FAKED RIOT STUFF GRAND
> REAL MC COY GET TIGER HUNT INDO-CHINA C.F.

Mike tore at his red hair. "Listen to the *ts'ao t'a ma-ti pi*! Here I risk limb and body and he says it's fake!"

"We're going after tiger."

"I hate cats."

We left for Indo-China by an old trimotor job. I had no trouble getting Mike to leave, as the Green Garbo had suddenly appeared at the hotel and wanted to know when she started to work in our picture.

17   the jungle Paris

VIET-NAM, as they call Indo-China now (they keep changing names in Asia as if the evil eye can be taken off a country by hiding its old names), is a jungle in revolt. The French are cynical, ironic, and some of them die bravely. The emperor—a worn-out rake—is not liked and he is protected by an army that is bleeding France at a rate that shocks the taxpayers back home. The French live in great islands of barbwire. They sleep armed during the night, and during the day make raids among native villages and into the mean jungle. It is a cruel, ugly war on both sides. And many of the big blond soldiers are former Nazi storm troopers enlisted in French regiments and sent out here to continue a war half under water and rare flowers.

Saigon, once the so-called Paris of the Orient, is a pretty picture framed in barbwire. One feels this an odd kind of savage frontier fort from our own Wild West, in the early days, with the Indians riding in on all sides and no hope of the U.S. Seventh to come galloping in at the last minute.

Business as usual, of course, with guns strapped to one's back, with armored cars and machine guns, with men tortured on both sides. Villages burned and women and children are prey for passing soldiers. There is little reason and no real sense, except that here we feel we can hold off the march of Asia and Marx and keep this corner as an entry into an Asia nearly lost. There is some reason for this some place in high places. But close up it is horror and evil against man, against nature.

Politics in print with good, solid, honest slogans doesn't look so neat when wrapped in barbed wire, dead men's entrails on a hot road, and women torn open with jungle knives.

CAMERAS IN PENANG

Asia boiled red hot the day we got to Penang with our cameras and asked the natives where we could film a tiger hunt. They were very polite and pointed inland to a jungle mess and Mike Murd said, "Oh, my aching back, you'd think a tiger would have more sense than to live back there in the muck. This ain't such a bad town."

For the Malay Peninsula, and the Indo-China jungle of temples and ruins, and of Angkor-Thom, it wasn't, but I wished I were finished with this daffy motion picture trip.

I hadn't heard from Turtle in some time and hadn't been paid in two months.

We began by hiring Jolson, "Jolie" as we got to call him. He was a sleepy-looking native who owned a collection of jazz records and offered to let me walk all over him when he discovered I had written the movie, *The Jolson Story*.

"Most best of all. I show some guide I can be. Food, girls, art work, and back-street black markets for wrist watches."

"A tiger hunt is all we want," said Mike, "and no tame cat in a barn. Real teeth, *this* long."

"How about a buffalo fight, an ellepahnt wrassling match?"

"What the hell is an ellepahnt?"

Jolson pulled out an imaginary trunk from his nose and begged a peanut for it.

Mike said, no dice, no ellepahnt wrassling . . . *just* a tiger hunt. Jolson said it could be done but would cost money, and he went off to arrange for it and a boat crew to take us upriver to call on the tigers. It all seemed very foolish to me . . . as a rock is a rock, and tiger is a tiger, and Mike said we had one in Hollywood "with rubber teeth and a weakness for doughnuts."

We had lunch on a terrace in a wave of big fans stirring the tired air, and the French all around us (slipping so badly as colonial masters) scratching their prickly heat and drinking small orders of a native brandy. The natives just stood around and chewed betel nut, and it was rather amusing, and sinister, to see their teeth painted black by the habit.

Mike called over a tall waiter in a nightshirt affair and a fez. The School of Paris had invaded Indo-China cooking, and the better American canned goods merchants have helped. (But no one, dead or alive, will eat Spam. A huge mountain of it simmers in the sun outside the town, left by some American mission.) There is no beef or mutton, and they use only the water buffalo as farming animals, which limits the menu.

OUR GUIDE "JOLSON"

The cooking is done on little charcoal pots and it's amazing how well they do.

I started Mike on a half-dozen little pancakes called *chavo*, made with fresh bean sprouts and mushrooms and shrimp, and of course a bottle of rice wine, *chiau*.

"Has it strong character?" Mike asked me.

"Tie your hair on tight."

"That stuff we had in Hong Kong ruined my back teeth . . . ate holes in them."

"Sip it from the little bowls and dream of peace and a poem."

"Does that help?" he asked, gulping a half-pint of the stuff.

"It brings you a soothing love of life, a contentment, a dream of tall, beautiful women, and a moon low enough to

BEB, THE NATIVE CHEF

bite, and the bamboo rattling in the wind and far off a singsong girl plucking a musical string."

"I think I better stop drinking, if that's *what* it does."

"The wise men are supposed to feel that way when they retire to drink and write poems in their old age."

"Skip it, character. I can't retire. I owe income tax and
back pay on two wives. What's solid food around here?"

"Easy, Mike—you can't rush these people."

"Look, I only came here to film a tiger hunt, not to spend
my ill-lived life mooning over perfumed booze."

I called in the *Beb* (as the native chef is called) and tried
out my *petit nègre* French on him, the sort of pidgin French
the natives seem to have invented, and after telling him his

grandmother was a goddess, I ordered lunch. And he went away feeling full of his manhood and joy in his peanut oils, and saying to us, *"C'est tout bon . . ."*

We began with a real treat, *ca giam dua,* a fish stew with pineapple. . . . Mike sighed after the meal, "It makes you want to be a beachcomber and lay around with them poems and broads and moonlight."

"Mike, we have a tiger hunt to film."

TOWARD THE TIGER

Back at the hotel we found Jolson biting into dimes he was handed by a group of natives.

"Native boys, they go with us. They pay me a dime each for getting job. Very good boys. All brother-in-laws."

"It's a big family," I said.

"I marry ten times."

"I lose," said Mike. "I'm just an amateur."

I could see that all the wives had been different. At first the natives all look alike. Then after a few days you can pick them out like faces of cowboy actors. They were Cochin-Chinese, Tonkinese, Annamites, the Cambodians whose grandpappies built the great stone jungle cities now in ruin, Siamese outlaws, and Malay Lolos and Mois. Most of them wore their hair very long, in coiled *chignons* and stuck full of pins, knives, combs, and, sad to relate, old rolled copies of American comic books, of which they are very fond.

"Is this all?" asked Mike.

"No," said Jolson, hiding his money in his mouth. "My wife and three childs come too."

"No dice," said Mike, who had a limited way of expressing himself.

"Must take wife, as I owe storekeeper a lot of money and

he will take wife if I leave her. And I like her now as much as he does . . ."

"Love is a four-letter word," said Mike, giving up. "We start at four o'clock, and I can't spend more than two weeks in the jungle . . . our producer, Chicken Fat (he seemed to bow in the direction of Culver City) wants us to go on to Ceylon and India . . . two weeks."

Jolson smiled. "We find tiger . . . very huge teeth like this!"

Mike narrowed it down to four-inch teeth. "I don't want them jumping over the cameras."

We went upriver in small boats with matting awning, and the boys working the long oars, the flies biting Mike and me, and Mike down with hives (the flies left the boys alone—no way to treat trusting strangers, I felt). It's a strange, brooding land, living in mist and heat and a past so strong it seems to leave the present as something foolish and something that will soon pass.

RUINS IN THE JUNGLE

The ruins around Angkor Wat are amazing, and they have drawn me three times to see them. There are almost eighty square miles of great stone ruins with the jungle covering, or trying to cover, everything with a net of creepers and wild green life. The temples are huge and powerful in form, and all over them one sees a message and the faces of Siva and Buddha. Even Mike was impressed as we stopped and looked, on the third day, at the great five-coned towers of the main temple at Angkor Wat. He stared at the gods; the Garounda, the bodhisattva, the Nagari, the devaraja, the Arpara. He followed the great carving, the dances, the marching lions, serpents, griffons and gods.

"Chum, this is something," he said, taking off his sun hat and rubbing his red hair. "I never saw anything like this. What a movie palace it would make on Hollywood and Vine!"

I love Mike, but at this point I was ready to break every leg on his second-best camera. He wandered off to buy a large linguiphallic symbol to send to our producer, Chicken Fat.

At dusk we watched the little dancing girls motion and twirl and turn. We sat very still except when we beat our necks to kill the night-brought insect life, or sipped the bot-tled Evian and Vichy waters that Jolson brought us and which

TEMPLE GIRLS

he watched us drink with pleasure (he got a franc back on every empty bottle).

We slept late and the next morning it was almost noon when we left the boats, ordered the porters under their bundles, and started up the green narrow path toward a village where they kept shaking in fear over a tiger reported in the brush somewhere and Red outlaws hunting French cops.

Two days later we were in a hill country having a little trouble breathing, and the village we came to was a collection of sticks and clay, and the natives were big grinning men with the black teeth of the nut-chewers. The headman was an old boy who carried big American silver dollars in his ears, and he said he might hunt tiger with us if we gave him a radio set, a cooking pot, and two dozen American comic books. As Mike was a comic book fan, and had a secret hoard of *Superman* and *Dick Tracy*, we managed it rather well, even if he was angry at giving up a first-edition, mint copy of *Blondie*.

TIGER IN THE BUSH

I had always had the impression that a tiger hunt is a thing of danger and daring, and as eager as a Republican in the feed bag. Jolson, however, managed it rather well. In an old tree he had a platform built and here we set up the camera and I looked over the ground plan so that if I had to match it in Hollywood, it would still make sense.

The only thing we didn't have was a White Hunter. To kill my own tiger was something I didn't care for. So Jolson had kept his left eye open for a White Hunter who had the permit and the big Express rifle, and could be brought in for the kill. In a sun hat and shot from the back, he would look enough like any Joyboy Glamourpuss, any movie star, who had never killed anything bigger than a jug of mountain corn in his native hills before they put shoes on him and told him that no woman in the world could resist his lovemaking.

On a clear, sunny day when the village folk at a dollar a head (less Jolson's ten per cent) were out in their white sheets and spears and tin cans, beating up the tiger country

THE TIGER VILLAGE

for a spore, into our camp came White Hunter. He was a thin, little old man with red eyes, a shaking hand, and a tall Express rifle. He was a Hungarian beachcomber called Buz-Zonder, and my first disappointment. I had expected a large, red-faced Englishman exiled from Oxford for some crime, or a tall Hemingway character with a Gary Cooper kisser, and a way of grunting calm, manly, hairy-chested words at our lily-white skins (a little heat-rashed) and our foolish efforts.

White Hunter (out of Budapest) wasn't like that at all.
He sat down and shook his head, "Wrong season for tiger,
but I need the money. How close you want him to come before I kill the beast?"

"Just within danger," said Mike.

"No danger . . . that's all nonsense . . . Tiger hunting
is safe as beef killing in Chicago."

"Look, Buz-Zonder, we have to make this look exciting."

"Then go after wild buffalo . . . much more danger than
tigers . . . I can take you to a place like Africa."

"I got a nice smelly goat," Jolie said.

"Is there any other kind?" asked Mike, who had to work
very close to the goat.

"You know," said the Hungarian. "Tigers like night for
hunting . . . I don't see how we're going to get any camera
stuff."

Mike roared, "I'm not a lousy sportsman . . . it's a job
we have to do. Get into the tree and Jolson will pep up the
natives to make more noise."

"Help me up," said White Hunter, "damnedest nonsense
to use trees. People get into habits and never change."

It was hot in the tree and I kept a finger in the Hungarian's
ribs to keep the old man from falling asleep. I was very worried this whole affair was going to turn out badly. The sun
was having trouble with a mist.

In about an hour we heard the natives growing louder and
Mike took a last look at a light meter. He kept making setups of the shot with his hands, and far down the field a striped
object strolled along and it was the tiger. He saw the goat
who was chewing on his own toes, and he walked slowly toward the goat.

"I'll fake the speed," said Mike, "so it will look as if he's
coming in fast."

The tiger walked over closer. Mike looked at White Hunter,
"Now?"

"Any time you want."

"He's getting close."

"Give him ten more yards."

"Better get him now . . . he looks bad."

"The molting season—losing his fur."

"Now, Zonder, now!"

THE KILL

The Hungarian put up his rifle, leaned against it, measured
something, rubbed his chin, nodded, pressed something, and
tiger did a quick dance, jumped in the air, came down on
his ear, and lay very still. His tail alone gave one, two, three,
little jerks before it, too, was still.

The Hungarian didn't even bother to look down again.
He put the rifle aside and took a cigarette from my pack and
asked me, "Is it true that Molnar left behind a new play?"

After which the natives came out and danced around the
tiger, and then Jolson got a big pole and tied the tiger to it,
and had two natives carry it around in front of the camera.
But they only did it once, no retakes, as they said it was very
foolish; we had a wheelbarrow for the camera, why not put
the tiger on that? Mike explained in American, the wheelbarrow is a very unromantic object, and as good comic-book
readers they should know it wasn't a tool anyone like Superman would be caught dead with.

"What kind of rug do you think our tiger will make?"

"He's got a few moths under his tail, and the shoulder is
mangy but a good taxidermist could fix him up."

Going downriver was pleasant. The boys rowed the boat
slowly and the river carried us, and the *Beb* made us special

food on his little charcoal pot, and at night under the pressure lamp I would wrap myself in a bug-proof net and read that all men led "lives of quiet desperation."

END OF HUNT

18 nightmare land

MALAYA is a bad dream, where one wakes up half-asleep, wondering if one is awake and not daring to put down a foot on the solid ground because things change so fast. Lives and property are wiped out so quickly that last night's planter who bought you a gin drink, while the recording machine played Gilbert and Sullivan, is dead today in an orchid-filled clearing, mutilated like a slaughterhouse pig. The spinning little native who served the drink can next week be hung up on a piano wire over an Army post with the proper reasons for it pinned to his long hair.

The British have more troops here than they have in Korea. They cannot maintain order, cannot wipe out the terror in

TOMMY IN THE JUNGLE

the jungles of rubber, in the red hills of tin. The natives are all in favor of the death-dealing jungle wolf packs and look with a thin smile at the white men in their prickly heat. There is, some place, a right and a wrong to it all, but on this dreadful peninsula reason goes quickly; one shoots at any sound or sudden move. And the English tommies think of cold beer and home. But rubber and tin are of great value in the world; they may be the deciding factor in victory of a yet-to-come global war. The more we dig and tap and ship, the safer somehow we feel. So there is no black and white in it. It's all mixed up. The fighting is dirty; natives tied together like onions in a market does not make one feel good; and native children keep out of white pools, playgrounds, schools. And then the body of a planter is brought in, like old garbage, from some jungle clearing and what was once a man is so broken and mean, one can only hate a little at first and then plan to leave quickly. It is so much easier to take sides when it's only a matter of principles and slogans and not people. All the rights in the world do not mend one wrong if one is in the spot seeing the wrong done.

BURMA IN THE MORNING

Burma could be renamed chaos, but we shot good footage there. It still rusts with the wrecks of tanks and cars and planes, left over from the last war. Its people and its temples are art forms easy to see and watch, but not to understand. Every man's hand and fist seems turned against his neighbor; warring factions, some of which make no sense to us, boil in the night and their rigid dead are found in the morning. Total disaster seems to be the only form of government that makes any sense here.

Rangoon is a delight to the eye, and if one's nose and stomach are not too weak, a pleasure to touch close up. The bombings still show scars of World War II. The Turf Club, former stronghold of the last thin, red line of Colonel Blimp and Mrs. Blimp, is now the clubhouse of the sporting youths among the natives. The native Navy is the big power in the land and their uniforms are from a musical comedy. The city is overcrowded—wretched in many slums but with the sun behind it and the day clear, it's in many ways a poem for which we lack the key words; but we can enjoy the music of just the sound and shape of it.

LORD BUDDHA SLEPT HERE

Bangkok is another place that seems left over from a kinder time, with its meaning never fully explained (as is best with beauty). The name Bangkok means "Where the Kok Tree Roots," and it sits in dignity on the banks of the Magnificent River (the Chao Phraya). Close to a million people live here. Its modern airfields make it the key to air travel in this part of the world. Planes seem out of place over the four hundred spires and wedding-cake roofs. To see us travel *over* the Temple of the Tree, the Temple of the Reclining Buddha, seems almost blasphemy.

Sampans drift and dart over the fruit-green jungle river. Canals cut the city into forms of modern art, bells ring too much but not too loudly, and everyone uses perfume and you don't mind it.

The city is a gesture of prayer to Lord Buddha. This city is his, as Mecca is a special city and certain places in Israel suggest Christ. The curtain of towers and spires all point up to where man is aching to reach some peace. Wat Arun, the Dawn Temple, lifts itself like stone lace five hundred feet from the roots of the growing plants and its porcelain points gleam like living fingertips raised in prayer.

The caves of Petchburi, where the great King Mongkut (they're all great later on) built a summer palace to taste flesh and prayer, sun and ideas, is filled with images of Buddha—the Enlightened One—in the poses and postures of true meditation. Of all of man's ideas of the godhead, and the peace inside, this one seems the most real, the most easy to grasp, without the hate of other sects, special rituals and brain-numbing dogma beyond reason and fact. Here myth has been stripped away; earthly ownership of Heaven, as one finds it in Europe in special cash-collecting hands, is lost in these caves where man sits, eyelids down, welcoming an inner calm. There are no bloody sainthoods, no booming voices of old hates, no wars and slaughters for myths or because your neighbor makes the sign of hope and faith in a way different than you do.

Buddhism on its home grounds becomes the best of all things. A gentle and flexible philosophy, tolerant of all things, kind to all ideas. One lives to collect *bunya*—merits—and to oppose *bapa*—sins. So one can reach nirvana, that last burst of truth that leaves one free from the sense of guilt in earthly passions. Here one can say, if God *is*, then the solid objects of the world can become an illusion, the starting point of a better understanding of what is and can be.

One knows here the law of karma and causation, cause and sequence, feels the atman, he who has neither form nor limit—who is infinite. We stand exhaling and inhaling, objects of repulsion and attraction, until we almost touch in these caves the nirvana of self-realization, but not quite.

MANGO LAND

The mood lasts until one walks out into the damp heat, until the drivers of the cars fight to drive you. And as you pass the tin-roofed American mission you hear the voices of the rice converts singing in flawed tones:

> *"Dare to be a Daniel,*
> *Dare to stand alone,*
> *Dare to have a purpose firm,*
> *Dare to make it known."*

Mangoes, bananas, and coconuts are in the stalls. Fighting fish swim in their little bowls and eat each other for the men who bet on them. Old men fly *gentlemen* kites covered with hooks and try to claw *lady* kites down from the sky. The hotel porter offers you Swiss watches, frigidaires, and RCA radios, cheaper than you can buy them at home. A group of saffron-robed Buddhists pass, smoking big black cigars, and the transport planes fly overhead as a kite falls, banging into the *chedis* spires of the tomb of Rama III.

CHRIST AND BUDDHA

We were living on the last of my traveler's checks—still no word from Turtle—no paychecks. Chicken Fat in Hollywood seemed to have forgotten us. I began to feel like a modern Flying Dutchman . . .

PAST PALK STRAIT

When you come through Palk Strait and coast into the Sea of Mannar, on your right, like a green ghost topped in mist with a hat of clouds, is Ceylon, looking just like the postal cards of it which tourists send home.

It had been a hard night for Mike Murd. He came up on

deck looking like a bargain-cellar item in old clothes, and he rubbed his face and mussed up what was left of his red hair.

"Boy, I should have a dollar for every drink I had last night."

I pointed toward the land. "Nogombo, and we get off next stop, at Colombo. Very fine clouds. Try them on your light meter."

Mike moaned. "Character, I don't know why I got talked into this clambake. We could have shot this picture in Jack Warner's back yard, with the Screen Writers Guild dressed up as natives."

"When you say *that*, smile," I said, and turned back to watch Ceylon walk toward us over the crayon-blue sea. Mike went down to try to get a Bloody Mary, a mixture of tomato juice, pepper, raw eggs, and secret herbs, which he claimed cured all ills of morning.

We landed among a group of *dhows* full of family wash and dogs and kids and went up to the hotel full of little Chinese figures of *Pu L'ai*, the popular local god of lechery. The bar was full of *pukka wallahs*, smoking reeking cheroots and drinking gin slings. It was very warm and moist, and we had a quick lunch, of three hours, on lobster *à la portugaise* and a *chaud-froid* of chicken and Ceylon crayfish. After which I put on my Gary Cooper shorts and my pith helmet out of Kipling and went out into the midday sun to find the mad local Englishman who represented the film company.

TROUBLE IN CEYLON

It seemed the Englishman had left for Egypt on the night plane with a wife; not his own wife, but a dear, kind creature who went along to spend the one thousand pounds that belonged to the film company and which we had hoped to share with him.

This meant trouble, so I cabled Chicken Fat for some cash. I got back to the hotel to find Mike wrapping himself around a huge *rijstaffel*—a great and wonderful dish.

"How much money have you on you, Mike?"

"About six bucks, Chinese."

"The local film branch is closed for repairs, and we haven't room rent."

Mike buried his face in the *rijstaffel*. "I shoulda stood with Goldwyn."

A small brown man whose stomach was chained together with two watches bowed to us and Mike said, "Meet Abul Zade-Pasha. A fellow American."

I looked at the fez on Abul's head and his Arab nose and his Turkish legs (they bend out at the knees) and said, "Don't invite him to dinner. We're short of cash."

Mike grinned. "Abul is the best tea taster and blender on the island, and in all Asia."

Abul nodded. "Best damn tea blender in the whole blasted world."

"Listen to the kid—he's hot stuff."

"I invent sixteen blends of tea last year. I can grade; fair, middle-fair, good, and fine. I grade tea into sixteen subdivisions *and*," he lifted Mike's cup of tea to his nose, "this is middle-fair, two plus mixed with a fine two minus. I can smell a good Pakistan, a little Sumatra oolong, and just a dash of real Darjeeling—Darjeeling, that's the best tea grown."

Mike looked at his cup of tea. "That's all in my cup of tea?"

"And the waiter's hair oil, and of course I could also smell the tea bag—long staple Hindu cotton."

"Mike," I said, "we're in trouble enough. We don't need a tea chef."

"Taster and blender. Look, Ceylon is just like Pasadena. Abul says we can grow *Thea sinensis* in Pasadena, even in the Rose Bowl."

I turned a little pale. "What's *Thea sinensis*?"

Abul smiled. "The Latin term for the venerable shrub that gives us black, green, and oolong tea. Black tea, as you know, is the fermented leaf, green is unfermented, and oolong is only half-fermented, just enough to get the good old enzymes flowing."

"Mike, we have to get some harbor shots and while it's nice to know Abul, I'm not interested in growing tea in California."

"You're the guy who wouldn't put ten dollars into the Ford Motor Company."

Abul shook his head. "You must understand, I know all teas: China, Japan, Formosa, Ceylon, and the caffeine content. I can measure it by just looking at the cup. My blends never

TEA GIRLS—CEYLON

have too much tannin, and I have sixteen little trees potted ready to take with me to California."

"No, Abul. We're just picture people."

"You will love these little trees. From Darjeeling, Assa, Nuwara Eliya . . . all the best kind of tea shrubs."

DEATH OF AN OLD, DEAR FRIEND

Mike took Abul into the bar and I went down to the cable station feeling very angry at the world, motion pictures, and tea. The cable office said no money had come in, and I went to the Planters Club where I had a nodding greeting from the club barman and a card from an English publisher admitting me to any planter's club in the world, for cash. It was *l'heure du cocktail*, and a White Russian refugee was mixing gin and greeting everyone.

At six o'clock I went back to the cable office. There was a cable from London:

TURTLE DIED LAST NIGHT CALLING OFF FILM MAC

It had only been a matter of time, I suppose, until Turtle's ulcers got him, but I wasn't prepared for it and I took it hard. He was an old friend and a very bright one and I had known him in my youth and that was something solid. Now he was gone and for some time I forgot we were stranded here. Mac had pulled out; Chicken Fat had seen it coming and left us high and dry.

I didn't want to see Mike just then, or his tea taster. I just wanted to have a drink at a bar alone and kind of have a few for Turtle . . . send Turtle damply on his way. I had reached the age where my friends had all dropped dead on the tennis court at forty or killed themselves or married money or retired to New Mexico ranches or Bucks County farms.

After a while I figured I was overdoing the mourning, and

I went down to the cable office and sent a cable to a newsreel man in Paris who had once been very earnest and heavy about getting me to make artistic travel shorts for him. I knew that most people who want you when others want you, don't need you when you're free, but it was worth a try.

At the hotel I broke the news to Mike and he said, "It's a crying shame. The wrong people always die. The rats never . . ."

Which seemed true, sometimes, but wasn't much of a help. At the hotel I tried to act as if we had lots of money. It was no effort for Mike at all. He signed for everything cheerfully. In the lobby I talked to an Indian Congress party man who said India was badly off and there was no hope of quick prosperity. But he was going to die trying to work things out and make India a great nation. The big cotton kings who now controlled a lot of the party, he said, knew they had to go easy on the stealing, and help the poor. But there were so many of the poor, weren't there? I said yes.

We slept late the next morning and I got up at noon and went down to the waterfront to see about a ship for home. Nothing in our price range was around.

A NEW JOB IN THE RAIN

That evening there was an answer from Paris:

> KNOW A CHAP IN SOUTH AFRICA WANTS SHORT
> TRAVEL SUBJECTS SHOT CONTACTING YOU DIRECT

I ran all the way, in the heat, to the hotel to break the news to Mike. Then we went back to the cable office, which was getting to know me. There was a cable from Capetown:

> WILL PAY PASSAGE ON PLANE TO CAPETOWN YOU
> AND CAMERAMAN TALK TERMS HERE SAM SUGAR—
> SUGAR FILMS

"Eating money anyway," Mike said.

Back at the hotel we waited for plane-tickets credit. The waiter brought in a tray of Cambodian fruits chilled in tamarind juice. Mike sighed and picked up his fruit fork.

I said, "Capetown, they say, is a great little burg."

Mike said, "I shoulda stood with Zanuck."

It was raining when we got to the airport. The rain came down as it can come down only in Ceylon. It came down in green sheets and silver sheets, and it knifed into the soggy runway and the gray collection of ant-eaten hangars, and it kept falling, and us sitting under a canvas roof hugging our camera gear and feeling very sorry for ourselves. The cable for our tickets hadn't come in yet.

Mike shook his head. "I hadda be an artist. I hadda come out here to hell-and-gone to get real backgrounds for pictures, so a lot of guys could have an excuse to buy popcorn and chewing gum when they go to see Lana Turner . . . blown up twenty times lifesize."

"Since when is that bad?"

"I hadda be an artist with a camera."

"Cheer up, Mike."

Mike wiped the rain from his hair. "I wonder what the boys are doing right now. The day crews are breaking. Maybe six good takes for the day, and they're seeing the dailies. And the star is saying he didn't like the dialogue, and the cutter is asking for the protection shots, and the producer isn't feeling so well, his gall bladder just gave birth to a groan."

"Sounds dull."

"Oh, shut up," said Mike. "Them was the good old days. Booze, broads, and box office. We never gave away a free dish, and Eric Johnson was just something to scare his mother with."

"Was it real fun making pictures, Mike?" I asked. "I

mean when somebody put his cap on backward and told the actors to be funny?"

"You writers ruined it. Came in with those words. No actor knew any words in the old days. You just hired a Hungarian whorehouse professor out of work and gave him a fiddle, and when it was a sad scene he played sad music, and when it was a gay scene, he played *schmaltz* with waltz stuff, and when the picture was finished we shipped it out and got back millions. No income tax, either. But you writers had to invent words, and now the public wants pictures to make sense. How the hell can Hollywood ever make sense!"

"Calm down, Mike. It's going to."

RAIN

"Them was the days."

A little brown man came across the field, almost swimming, and said the plane was taking off, as the rain was breaking, and would we please take our seats, the cable okaying payment for our seats had come.

THE TIN BIRD WEST

The plane, a big silver bird, was smoking and snorting at the end of the field, and we waded to it and got in and sat down and wiped our faces. The rain looked worse than ever, and the propellers beat it like eggs in a dish. But the two old R.A.F. boys at the controls, being very Kipling and proper, gave the field crew a signal, and we waddled like a duck across the bog. And after a long, long time we got an inch off the ground and stayed there and kept going into the mist. Once a Chinese temple passed us, and once I saw a yellow horse through a hole in the mist about ten feet above us on a hill. I shut my eyes and tried to fool myself that I had been every place and done everything twice, so it didn't matter if we crashed.

After a long while Mike said we were over the sea, and sure enough, occasionally the sea would wink up at us. The big storm hit us then, and I don't think there is any place like a plane in a storm at sea for feeling how small and short life is.

The storm went on through the night, and we sat feeling very glum, and Mike was wondering what the boys in the back room of the Brown Derby back in Hollywood were having. And I thought of Turtle and the stuff we had kicked around.

One of the R.A.F. boys came toward us and Mike said, "Can't something be done about this storm?"

"What storm, old chap?"

Mike said, "I shoulda stood with the King Brothers."

It was a long flight and I read an old cookbook I had picked up.

> *A Mortreux of Flesh,* 1450 A.D. [I read]. Take pork and seethe it enough; and take it up and skin (*bawde*) it, and chop it and grind it and put it in a mortar; and cast thereto grated bread, and then draw the same broth through a strainer. And temper it with ale, and put all in a pot, and let it boil, and allay it with yolks of eggs. And then let it boil no more. And cast thereto powder of ginger and salt, and put it in dishes, in manner of mortars (*mortrewes*) and cast thereto powder of ginger, and serve it forth.
>
> *Bruet of Almayne,* 1430 A.D. Take almonds and draw a good milk thereof with water. Take capons, coneys, or partridges; cut up the capon, or kid, or chickens, or coneys; the partridge shall be whole. Then blanch the flesh and cast on the milk, take lard and mince it and cast thereto; take and mince onions and cast thereto enough; put cloves and small raisins thereto; cast whole saffron thereto; then put it to the fire and stir it well. When the flesh is [done] enough, set it off the fire, and put thereto sugar enough. Take powdered ginger, galingale, cinnamon (*canel*) and temper it with vinegar and cast thereto. Season it with salt and serve forth.

The sandwiches on the plane were dreadful, so I had to stop reading the cookbook, and I dozed.

19   the black land

ONE of the paradoxes of our time is the fact that Africa is a fine place to live, except for the Negro. The black man has lost his birthright, and lynch-mob minds and Nazi methods run most of Africa. And yet, one knows the Negro will not be kept down forever. Dreadful will be the day when he is forced to take over . . .

Africa is like a beautiful punch in the nose to me. I am always glad to see it and always find new facets on its face to admire and enjoy. I had been all over it in my daffy youth, and once hunted mangy lions there with a White Hunter who told bigger lies than a book publisher's blurbs. I used to drop small talk about my safari out of Zanzibar into the Ugago country, and into the poison-green Unyanyembe jungle. But I would often forget to say I had gone there with a rich man's son who was trying to cure the drinking habit; he did, but then the native beer is rather hard for white men to drink.

I was telling all this to Mike as the plane rushed us at a fearful rate toward Capetown and a man we had never seen called Sam Sugar, of Sugar Films.

Mike was bored. He sat on his spine in the plane seat and watched the clouds chase each other over the Mozambique Channel.

He said, "It's all the same to me, character. Give me two old lions on a lion farm in Glendale, and enough palm leaves to blot out the phone wires and I can shoot a jungle epic any place."

"Nothing at all here?"

Mike was polishing his lens. "Peachy clouds. Get a nice yellow filter on 'em and we'll get some fine stuff."

"Damn the clouds."

"Wake me up when you see a Zulu," said Mike and turned over and went to sleep. After three wives and a six-year contract at Metro, Mike knew there was nothing worth while left in life.

A neat little Englishman on my right smiled at me and asked, "Cinema chaps?"

I admitted it and the little Englishman introduced himself. "Major Gwelo. Been back to London for a binge. Nothing tiptop left there. The old place has gone stale and colorless. Nothing left of the old glow. Shoddy, I would say . . ."

"England is changing."

"Looked forward to it, you know, but it's flat. Much better when we came back in the old days when I took the Prince of Wales out for a hunt."

I said, "The Prince used to be a good shot."

"Pretty steady at fifty feet, no good closer. But a nice chap. Doesn't hunt any more, I hear."

"Have you been taking hunting parties out a long time, Major Gwelo?"

"Thirty years. Taken them all in my time. Blasted titles, once a party of Chicago bootleggers. Rum chaps, hit elephants with machine guns and bombed apes with hand

LAKE TANGANYIKA

bombs. Fun though. Got some cat—we don't say lion here you know, just cat . . . Yes, got some cat at Ujiji and by Lake Tanganyika. Had fifty-three Bagamoya boys, three Remingtons, a brace of number-ten Reillys, and a 557-bore Express. Did things proper in those days. Cost a lot of tin— money, you know. Now they want one cat rug and some lechwe or eland horn, and five hundred feet of film in color. Class all gone out of the business."

THE MAN WHO KNEW HEMINGWAY

He sighed and took a bottle of pinch-bottle out of a linen bag and filled two small silver cups and we drank.

"Great fun in the old days. Old Ernest used to be along. Writing chap, you know, all hair on his chest and always sweating in joy over the kill."

"Hemingway?"

"That's the lad. What ever became of him?"

"Still writing."

"Anything cozy in it, any tin?"

"He's done all right. Was he a good hunter?"

"Fairish. A little too fancy. All proper and outfitted like a sports shop, and a little too earnest . . . Ernest—joke—what?"

I joined in the laughter of English humor.

"Not a bad chap at all. But all this talk now about blood and death, and grace under pressure, and the manhood. You think the old boy was worried about *it*? Good bottle man, however; drank only the best and passed it around. Doing well, you say?"

"Doing fine."

"Well, he got out of it in time. Nothing much left in the hunting line any more. Even the elephant tussocks beyond Kenya and Handeni almost bare. Permits now to kill, like it was a bloody East End ration line buying eggs. Natives just sitting around on their pandanus mats, eating plantains and papaws, and dreaming of the day when they can afford a wireless set. And the stinking Boers—nasty, aren't they now?"

We sat and drank pinch-bottle and admitted the world was going to hell in a hack, and that Africa was becoming too damn neat and political.

Capetown from the air is impressive. Table Mountain lives

up to its name, and gray clouds like shapes out of modern art veil it from time to time. And it's a great sight that neither age nor surfeit spoil to see the point of the Cape of Good Hope and watch the crayon-blue Atlantic Ocean meet the deep blue of the Indian Ocean . . . the meeting of these two great bodies of water would impress anyone, except sleepers like Mike Murd.

We landed and I shook hands with White Hunter, the Major Gwelo, and promised to drop over for a spot after tiffin. A thin, tanned man with a large head stood behind a wire fence at the airport. He had a proper Public School stance (which means private school in England). He came toward us as Mike wrassled the cameras out of the plane.

"Sugar is the name. Sam Sugar. Sugar Films. 'The Sweets of the Show,' ha ha," he said, holding out his hand.

I shook the hand and introduced Mike and he said he was happy to see us.

"Always happy to see anyone from Hollywood. Spent a wonderful week end there with Sam Goldwyn and Hedda Hopper. Love that Hopper."

Mike said, "So we're working for you?"

"I do hope so. Things are slack in the cinema field . . . lots of political excitement. The Boers have taken over, lots of Nazi stuff, and keeping the black man and Indian in his place, but we're hopeful it's just a passing thing. Great theaters here, and England needs films badly."

CAPETOWN HOLLYWOOD

"Any studio space and lights and props?" Mike asked.
"Let me show you."

We went out to a battered Bentley car and piled in and tucked the cameras away in the back. Sam Sugar drove as if he were in a tank that could go through anything. We found

CAPETOWN

out he had driven a tank during the war, from Bengasi to Tobruk, and had been captured at Bu Ngem and escaped and joined the underground in Palestine—the *Irgun*—and fought the Arab Legion. And now was back trying to really make travel pictures for the world market. He had plenty of go and dash but seemed short on cash and space. His studio had a huge sign: SAM SUGAR, SUGAR FILMS, "THE SWEETS OF THE SHOW," and a large garage that had once stored fish, from the smell of it. There were some lights, two cameras that should have been in museums, and an office with a large iron safe that Mike said he expected Stanley and Livingston to step out of when Sugar opened it.

He took out a small tin box and counted out fifty pounds.

"That's the cash on hand, boys. I'm willing to split it three ways right now."

"You're a right guy," said Mike. "But why should we take your dough if this is the last of it?"

"Well, if we can shoot a two-reeler of Capetown and get some sound on it, I can sell it for a hundred pounds to an English company, spot cash. And we'll split the extra fifty the same again. With that we can go upcoast to the diamond country . . . make some shorts and keep just ahead of debt . . . and at last get enough to make a full feature by the time we reach Bechuanaland. *If* you lads like the idea."

Mike put his arm around Sam. "This is a right guy. Sam, we're in business if this other Democrat votes right."

I did and Sam Sugar said this called for a beano, or rather a big lunch, and he took us in the rattling Bentley across town and up the coast where we sat on a huge porch looking out over the great sweep of the ocean that drove and drifted against the African shore.

THE BOERS IN POWER

Nobody has written much about the food in South Africa, and I found out why. Like certain secrets in the life of Chaucer or the lost paintings of El Greco, one could spend a lifetime and just scratch the surface. Germans and the French and English and the East Indians and the natives from the Kaffir and Zulu tribes have all put their spoons into the national cooking and the result is fine but confusing. The natives are a great race for playing around with corn. They eat the mealies, or cobs, raw, ripe, green, yellow, roasted, or fresh. They make a strong and fearful Kaffir beer that had sparks coming out of Mike's eyes. They cook their peanuts (called ground nuts here) instead of roasting them, and their soda pop is a sour-milk brew called *Amasi.*

The Boers are great pigs of eaters, and they cook lamb and mutton a great deal and eat the damn stuff with a hot mustard. Curries and kedgerees are very good and popular, as we found out, and skewered meat is to be had at its best all over the country. They use the capsicum and the *Brinjal* eggplant.

Sam Sugar bought us a great meal. I remember something yellow being made with raisins, spiced with lemon, saffron, and tamarind. Tripe of steer filled with pickled beef and pork, Dutch chicken pie that had white wine, brandy, and ham and eggs in it.

There was also a huge plate of Dutch apple fritters called *applepoffertje*, a real treat, boiled in deep fat. And the end of the meal had the flowers and stem of some water lily called the *bredie*, ground fine and cooked with onions, lemon juice, and mutton fat . . . fried a Vandyke brown and served.

Then the cape gooseberry and *granadas* and mangoes for fruit. The wines were local and good, but *not* out of this world. The best is a *Drankenstein*, a fair *La Gratitude*, and a native Dutch fire in small glasses, just before rising, called *Van der Hum.*

"It sure makes you hum," Mike said, getting up slowly.

"It makes you roar."

TO LAKE BANGWEULU

On this kind of fare we shot out a two-reeler in three days and went north as soon as Sam, the delight of our life, got a letter of credit from the English film company. We did a short film on the diamond industry at Kimberly, and then one on the native and white life at Johannesburg, where Sam had relatives who took us in and fed us. Northern Rhodesia looked like a bad place to crash, so we came down at Lake Bang-weulu, where Sam had an uncle who ran a trading post

and spent most of his time reading Mark Twain in Dutch.
"Huck Finn" sounded very funny in Dutch (but not funny
enough).

We hired a dozen lake boats and some native boys and
went out into the reeds and we photographed hartebeest,
reedbuck, giraffes, *and* buffaloes (not the kind on the nickel).

LAKE BOATS

It was not as much fun as it sounded. We shipped out the
last reel of film and Sam went along with it, so we sat down
to wait for some cash to appear while we ate saddle of reedbuck (which is as good as venison, when there isn't too much
of it). And *chapatties*, the Hindu unleavened bread, made
by our Moslem cook, a very hefty, gay native gal who giggled
like mad when Mike called her "Honeychile."

We sat two weeks in the lake reeds with Sam's uncle and
I read *Roughing It* and *Life on the Mississippi* in Dutch. It
didn't taste the same somehow. Mike amused the cook, Honey-

chile. He even got her to try to make spareribs, Southern style. For some reason, Mike treated the cook as if she were from New Orleans, and he would spend hours on *you-all* and *sure-nuff* talk to her, while she giggled and tried to keep her face veiled. She didn't understand a word of English, and Sam's uncle refused to help Mike's routine in Dutch.

Then the cook's husband appeared, a large red-faced Turk who peddled tinware to the natives. Mike used to sit sadly outside their mud hut, while the Turk played on his tin flute a sad, sad tune and Honeychile smoked a waterpipe and giggled with joy at her lord and master.

"If only that Turk would stop playing that flute."

"It's love music," I said.

Mike said, "I don't see what Honeychile sees in that mug. I wouldn't even use him to play character parts in Westerns."

"We ought to get the uncle to fix the radio set and see if there is any news of a plane crash."

But the uncle said he was sorry. The last of his radio tubes had been given away to one of the wives of a Kassama chief. She wore it around her neck as a jewel.

SAM FLIES BACK

Just at dusk the old trimotor Ford settled down in the mealie patch behind the trading post, and out stepped Sam Sugar, his clothing new, and Bond Street at that.

"Lads, we've hit the old jackpot."

"What happened?"

"I ran over to London by air and couldn't reach you."

"You look like a store-window dummy."

"My tailors in London dashed these off. Lads, they love our films in London, and I've an order, with a lot of cash attached to it. We're going into Uganda and do a short feature in color of Victoria Falls, and then follow the Bahr el Abyad into the Nile, and past the Sudan and the Kordofan Plateau into Egypt."

"That's a big order."

"Come and take a look at our new color camera."

It was a very beautiful camera, and a very wonderful evening, with wine instead of native beer, and Mike made a great speech in basic English on the future of the art of the cinema. "There just isn't any way to stop the lousy industry . . ."

The next morning we began to pack the plane and get everything ready for the trip. I was a little worried about the wild country ahead. I'm the kind of traveler who doesn't like to get rough with nature. I took Sam aside.

"I'm not going chicken on you, but what about gasoline and film and food and all that ahead?"

"I've got relatives all over this country. Don't you worry. There isn't going to be any trouble this trip. There are five thousand gallons of petrol stocked up near the Blue Nile, and I've orders to use all I need."

"Will the plane last?"

"It's lasted almost fifteen years . . . why should it stop now?"

I had no answer so I went to pack.

NAZIS IN AFRICA

The British are holding on to what they can in South Africa, but in the Union of South Africa it appears they have lost their grip for good. The Boers have stayed on and hung on, these dull, bigoted farmers, and they are taking over. The goodness of Jan Christiaan Smuts is forgotten. The Nationalists are top dog and their private army, the *Skietcommando,* modeled directly on the Nazi SA and Hitler SS troops, has stripped "Her Majesty's" insignia from all uniforms. The second Queen Elizabeth's textbook must be translated into *Afrikaans*, the Boer tongue.

Just three hundred years ago the Dutch came here in the first of their ships, the *Goede Hoop*. They took over from the aborigines, killing and enslaving. Today two million Boers sit on eight million blacks. *Apartheid*, white supremacy, is the godhead of the *Afrikaner*, as the Boer likes to call himself. The local newspaper, *Afrikaners Die Burger*, sounds a great deal like Hitler's and Goebbels' scandal sheets. It says Africa belongs to them and the black man is in his place—a permanent "hewer of wood and drawer of water" as it says in the Bible. Most evil in the world, you will find, is based on holy text by bigots in power; any holy text, any bigot. The true road to fascism is popular here: Anti-Negro, anti-Jewish, anti-Indian, anti-English, and of course anti-American ("go back and clean up Harlem, go free the Scottsboro boys").

The half-caste is also a second-class citizen. The Dutch and British blood in them is enraged, and the police beat them badly. They have Gandhi's son among them, but they will not too long, they swear, take it sitting down. Civil war is not just talk. The Boers may again have to retreat into their wagon squares and fight off something that they created— hatreds.

Every day I read "experts" who have it all figured out— what is wrong with Africa. They give hundreds of reasons and thousands of pages to details. But any honest man can figure it out in five minutes: *The white men stole Africa, a very rich place, from the black men and they don't want to give it back.* You can "expert" all you want, but basically that's it.

Africa, rich and wonderful, belongs to the black men, and they haven't got it. The British kept hold of everything but they were very fair about it in many ways and were legal and

BOERS HAVE SLAVES

helpful in many forms. But the British are fading out all over the world and the Boers and the others aren't giving an inch or playing it politely.

The Boers have degraded the blacks. They are herded into sickening slums, they are clubbed and beaten by brutal police, the courts fine them to poverty and jail them. They are exploited just like slaves, they are diseased, hungry, in rags. And they are turning mean. At night all houses are locked, all men go armed, and every night a few whites get their throats cut. And someone is punished for it—anyone with dark skin —it doesn't matter who. The full racial laws of the Nazis are enforced here. Hitlerism lives here—is a vital force. The

white men walk, the kings of the earth, but they sweat at
night and look worried for all their dirty, brutal power.

The stink of native slums, the sight of native disease, the
beating and killing of dark men, are not pretty. The explo-
sion has to come. Either the Boers will kill millions of natives
(they're prepared to) the way the Germans murdered twenty-
five million people in their camps, or the black man will rise
in some fury, in some warped version of Marxism or thugism
or mumbo-jumbo, in some holy war of spear and fire and
rape . . . And we shall sit back in horror and say that the
nature of man is an amazing thing . . . The colored races of
the world are rising from their long sleep. They don't care
who frees them . . .

20   the shores of North Africa

NORTH AFRICA saw Romans, rimmed in bronze, fight elephants here; saw many wars now forgotten. It's ready for more. Algeria, Morocco (both parts under Franco or France) are boiling like the local puddings in their copper pots. From Colomb-Béchar across the Sahara to Fez, to Safi, new graves are again being dug alongside crosses of the American adventurers into North Africa.

The Moslems are tired of being under protectorates. They sit proud in their fleas and filth, descendants of the Prophet, and even if the sultan has fluorescent-lit palaces at Rabat, they are wanting out. The *Résidence Générale*, an old hand at hanging Arabs with piano wire, is worried. Nationalism, that popular twentieth-century disease, is all over the world and has badly infected North Africa. Big profits and low taxes have lured Frenchmen here, and not one wants to turn the grab bag over to its owners.

One of the native independence groups called *Istiglal* wants to do it without bloodshed, but the followers of the Grand Mufti and his fanatics want throats cut. Moslem nationalism has not been so strong since the Turk was almost master of the world in those few generations after the death of the Prophet.

The Arab is poorly off, exploited by his own rulers and the village landlords. But he wants to be ruled again by his own, beaten by his own, killed by his own sultan's bow strings. He is willing to offer his neck freely to the native despot, for his nationalism is marching. The tanks and troops and police may beat in heads, arrest, and paste up orders, but the street-corner Arab shrugs it all off and moves on slowly when he's beaten on the back with the cop's baton. The jails are full, but arms and bloody talk are filtering in. Oil for the machines of the West has made Arab leaders rich . . .

TURN LEFT FOR TUNIS

The shrill natives of North Africa do nothing by half, more by thirds as I found out when I tried to get all my baggage off the bus from the airfield at Tunis. The extra cameras were there but not the film, and someone had walked off with my second-best umbrella. It was 120 in the shade and it was only just after dawn, so I knew it was going to be hot. I was supposed to wait at the hotel for Mike, who was some place inside the desert country filming native life, and I was to look it all over and write a text to fit the needs of the footage.

I went to a *souk*, as the native shop is called, and cheapened a good umbrella.

The shopkeeper pulled his burnoose and the flowing *hlafa* tight around his fat body and saw I was an easy mark.

"Three hundred franc."

"Fifty."

He had me now and knew it. He spit politely at the women passing covered in white *sarouels,* and *malafara* over their faces.

AT THE AIR PORT

"The grave of my father would rot away if I lost so much on the deal. Hundred and fifty francs for the sunshade."

A soft-drink seller passed with his brass pot, and I bought drinks, and we settled down to cheapen the sunshade. I got it for eighty francs, twice what it was worth. I couldn't spend the time getting it for what it was worth. I was due for lunch with the Burtons, who were important in the English set.

The Burtons had read one of my books, and I had met them in London at a play of mine that was running there, and so I had accepted an invitation to visit them in their summer place in Algiers. They did not live in the *Kasbah*, as most people thought. The *Kasbah* stinks, reeks, runs, and climbs up narrow streets (it's not romantic in any way). They lived in the quarter known as *Mustapha Supérieure*, a very neat, white, overheated place with air conditioning, swimming pools, and livers spoiled by consumption of too much scotch-and-splash.

There is an English church and English hospital and an American gas station where you can get dope (or so my driver told me. He may have been lying).

The Burtons, in white, were waiting for me. They had a neat place known as a salon-salle-à-manger. And little stoves called "Salamanders," that turn one's nose blue in the cold season, as I well knew from the old days.

The male Burton smiled at me showing the twice lifesize teeth of all Englishmen.

"This is fine of you to come," he said.

"It is getting hotter."

Mrs. Burton, young and very stylish, suggested I get some whisky and hot tea into me. Englishmen have proved that while this mixture may not cool you off, it will certainly put you in a condition of not caring about anything. The world is changing, but people not native to the tropics go on as if it were still 1907.

"Lunch in an hour," I was told. "Native, in your honor."

I groaned and went up to shower. A native meal is often sixty courses and Moslem dietary laws, while very good, often scare an American stomach. I showered, drank my whisky, telephoned the airport.

"We have not found yet the lost things. Have you visited our markets? *Alors, revenons à nos moutons.*"

I lost baggage and camera film . . .

NATIVE FOOD

Downstairs the servants in white were waiting. I enjoyed the meal. The table was low and we sat on the floor on mats and cushions. The male Burton grinned. "It's a special treat for us to show you this way of eating."

I rubbed my flanks and nodded. We started with *pastillas,* thin, baked dough filled with eggs, meat, and liver, also almonds. A side dish was *couscous,* just a grain porridge which everyone eats here. *Samak,* a Tunisian fish appetizer; *schorba,* a soup flavored with mint; *el anzah miswi,* which is good until you find out it's young roast goat; and after it, *tchechuka,* a green dish with eggs; *tamiya,* bean balls, and *fakha taza,* special fresh fruits. We ended with *kakwa,* which is a North African coffee that is a story in itself and eats holes in the lining of the stomach.

"Oh," I said, "I better go see the American consul."

"Not in this heat. Opera company playing tonight. You come with us. The American chap will be there. How about a gin-and-tonic?"

I let him talk me into it.

The Burtons dressed for the opera as if they were in London or Paris. I brushed the last of my Beverly Hills clothing and went along. It was a hot night. The opera was in Italian. The company was French, the composer was German, the costumes were Spanish. Everyone loved it, even the lady singers with flea bites on their legs. As for me, opera is better than it sounds, as someone once said.

I said to the Burtons, "Where is the American?"

"We're meeting him after the opera at a little native place. Real native food. Just for you."

Mrs. Burton purred, "We don't mind going to all this bother for a guest like you. Maybe someday you'll put it all

SINGER AMONG THE FLEAS

into *Gourmet* magazine. No one gets the real native food out
here any more, unless they know where."

It was a real native place. The goats lived in the dining
room. The food was very good. We had *el bkeila*, beans and
spinach; *bamya bourani*, chicken and okra; and *savadia*, fish
with lemon. I found the American behind a pair of polished
bifocals. He didn't seem pleased to see me when I told him
I wanted to film North Africa and Egypt. And I hoped Mike
would be safe.

"Damn it, why don't you Hollywood people stay at home?
It's a native habit out here to throw cameramen in jail. Well,
they'll not shoot him."

"I know, but he's only got one nose and two ears. If they cut them off, he'll be a drug on the market."

"Well, I daresay they'll never go that far. Unless he's in the habit of violating virgins."

"You forget, he's from Hollywood."

"Then there is no danger."

I said the foundations of the country were being shaken and promised to go along with Bifocal to the native market the next day. He was a nice boy of forty-two who had been to Harvard and was related to Hoover, and hoped to get rich enough to retire some day to Philadelphia.

The native market was impressive. "A riot of color," said Bifocal, coining a phrase right before my eyes. I tasted a

TRAPPIST MONK FROM STAOUELI

loquat called *nefles* and disliked a vegetable marrow called *courgettes*. Mutton hung around to keep the flies happy, and the women in their white pants and covered eyes chewed watermelon seeds and spit courteously on all Christians. The wine was a pleasure. Monks, big, sensual, bearded Trappists from the Staoueli monastery, sold it. *Rouge, blanc, or rosé. Vin ordinaire* at two francs a bottle.

BLACK-MARKET BOY

It was hot and the mosques, minarets, and flat-topped roofs reflected the heated brass air, and it boiled down on us. Bifocal went off to go to work and I found myself facing a little fat Frenchman eating slices of *mouna* cake and letting the crumbs nest in his beard.

"How is your opera company doing?" I asked, recognizing him.

The opera manager bowed. "Ah, last night . . . what a night. I sent the cash home by *bureau de poste*."

"There will always be a France," I said.

"An *apéritif*?"

"No native food," I insisted.

"*Ah bon! Le bon vin, le bon vin.*"

He was a nice guy.

"Here it is fine," he said, "but in the back lands! They kill you as soon as look at you. The jails, worse than our *gare de chemin de fer*."

"You've been in jail here?"

"Dozens of times," he said proudly. "Fleas no longer touch me. My stomach is cast iron. I can sleep with *joie de vivre* with a stone for a pillow."

"Do they really cut off a nose or an ear?"

"Only on the black market." He leaned over me and said

softly, "Would you care for a hot Matisse, or a ton of soya beans?"

"No, thank you."

"*Jeunes filles,* a Steinway piano good as new, a mink coat that once belonged to Rita Hayworth?"

"No."

"Let us have another drink. I show *les distractions* in this town. Let us grab a *rapide* for the native section. There is a street called The Fish Market . . . We could make a film there."

"No, I'm just doing travel stuff."

"Why did I not think of this before! I have a whole opera company! We will film an opera here. You know Ali Dore Schary at Metro-Golem-Mayer?"

TOWARD EGYPT

I went back to the Burtons and let myself in and was thankful it was too late to have a native lunch. The next morning Mike's voice was on the phone. An hour later and he was drinking the Burtons' best scotch and scratching himself in their best chair.

"Fella, you ain't lived unless you've been in the can in this country. You wouldn't believe it. No democracy at all."

"Why in the clink?"

"Just my feelings. I took some pictures of native women. They don't like it. We got out fast. I said I was FDR's nephew."

The male Burton came in. "I say, I'm recalled to Cairo— trouble there again. You chaps can have this place as long as you need it."

"Could we go with you?" I asked. "We need transport."

"I'm leaving in a special plane in half an hour. Could get you on it."

I shook his hand hard. I looked him in the eye. We shared the White Man's Burden (boredom) and knew it.

An hour later we were flying over high sand hills with only a stray camel to stare up at us. The male Burton sat and read Orwell's *Animal Farm*.

Mike sucked on a bottle of *tambrahandi* made from palm-tree juice, and I sat and wrote a secret report to the Screen Writers Guild: "The Film Situation in North Africa."

The news from Egypt was bad on the radio.

FELLAH, EGYPT

21   King Farouk is in exile

A KIND of evil stirs over Egypt. In Cairo one can almost see it, taste it. The mobs that went into a four-thousand-million-dollar looting, burning orgy in the streets some time ago are just resting. The burned houses and hotels are still around. The fanatics of the Moslem Brotherhood, sparked by the Grand Mufti (Hitler's friend who bribed his way out of French hands), are ready to cut any throat. They are packed into the reeking slums behind the Moslem Divinity School. The soldiers in their green uniforms, simple *fellahs*, will not stand up against them. The dirty corruption ring that is the Wafd party is very strong and wants a holy crusade and more graft.

Once they said, King Farouk, fat and poker-faced, in his special Cadillac, "waits for something to happen before deciding just how he can act. People say he is against the Wafd, the fanatics. He wants the British to leave the Canal Zone; he needs a unity of Egypt and the Sudan. Some doubt he wants a clean, honest government, an education system, more land and help to the *fellahs* in the stink of the Nile mud, less taxing of small people, more taxes paid on untaxed incomes of the rich. Neither side trusts the fat playboy, the sensual goat." Now he is gone.

Meanwhile the beggars grow scabbier, the little Citroens run along through the streets at reckless speeds, and the land that is Egypt doesn't appear very happy. The pashas come and go. Rule and pocket their loot, come and try to make order

THE BABIES SUCK UP DISEASE

out of fanatics, leave and give it up. And the Nile floods
every year, and brown and heavy goes to the sea carrying its
wedge-shaped sails. And the brown babies stand knee-deep
in the flood and suck up disease and watch the old stones of
forgotten dynasties across the way.

Riots are not taken too seriously in Egypt. This new one
had just been fun; a few dead, a few American women in-
sulted, and two Buicks burned in the street. The best hotels
had been burned by the mobs some time ago.

CAIRO INTERVIEW

I was staying at the New Continental Hotel in Cairo, sleeping pretty well in the heat that drove out Moses, except for
the local belly dancers in the roof garden over my room that
shook the building with their talents. I was cutting and edit-
ing a film during the mornings, and afternoons I went with my
English friends across the Nile to the remains of the Gezira
Sporting Club (it had been more or less pogromed in a riot)
to watch the Empire Builders kill themselves over cricket
on the imported greensward. It was very nice to sit in the
shade with a glass of gin-and-tonic and look past the pink
young Englishman toward where the three pyramids of Giza
just sneered at us across the brown air.

A black boy in shining dazzling white came up to me, I
was wanted inside. A little man with large teeth and a flat
head under a modern straw hat stood there smiling at me.

"I am from *The Egyptian Mail.* I would like an interview."

"I haven't anything to say."

"Is it true you are going to turn Egypt's motion picture
industry into another Hollywood?"

"No."

"Don't you think we, here, are able to make anything
Hollywood does better?"

"No."

"Isn't there a great future in Egypt for making great classic motion pictures?"

"No."

I thought it was a fine interview, short, to the point, and honest. The paper the next day carried a glowing text of what I hadn't said at all. "Egypt was the coming art center of the world." Its studios would furnish the films of the future, and I was going to direct a picture on the life of the great Pharaoh Amenhotep III and his ivory and papyrus court at the Lower and Upper Kingdoms.

I issued a statement that if I made a picture in Egypt it would be about the Jews crossing the Red Sea, which was on my part a mistake, as the Jews in the Negev desert had beaten the pants off the Egyptian Army. I was sitting on the terrace of the hotel brushing off the kings of Egypt who were standing around begging for *baksheesh*! when Burton, my English friend, came up to me swinging his cane.

"I say, that wasn't a smart thing to say. You know everybody has beaten the Egyptians in battle for four thousand years. I have a friend at the press office at *Sharia Eloui*, and I've talked it over with him and I think if you went on the air things might be worked out."

"The air?"

"The Egyptian Broadcasting Company."

"What can I say?"

"Oh, you could talk about native food, as it strikes you."

I looked at the male Burton, but I saw he wasn't kidding —just sitting there very proper holding his cane; which I now saw was an umbrella rolled with great skill. (It never rained in Cairo and no Englishman ever unrolled his umbrella, not even in London's worst storms.)

Somehow, no matter where travelers go, people think they come to eat native food. I've eaten everything in my time from the eyeballs of camels to sheep tripes dipped in honey and mare's milk. In Cairo I was quite willing to stay on pigeon and watermelon, but I could see it was not to be.

"I suppose I could talk on native art," I said.

"Good chap," said the male Burton. "They'll set up a nice table for you today. They give a big chop once a week for newspaper chaps."

"Thank you," I said.

It was a fine lunch held at the Metropolitan Hotel. There was of course the usual roast goat which is also sold as lamb, mutton, chicken, and duck. I never saw a whole duck or chicken in Egypt. But they did have *yaghnet kawanees jaj bersharia*, chicken giblets and vermicelli, which under another name is very popular in Italy. There was also an Armenian dish, *midia dolma*, stuffed mussels; and my favorite, *mozemma badenjan*, baked eggplant with tomatoes. When you remember that tomatoes were an American plant called "love apples" and thought to be poison a few hundred years ago, it's rather amazing that the Near East has grown so fond of the soft red fruit.

I spoke on the radio of food, love, letters, and the progress of mankind toward his doom. It was an odd mixture, but they seemed to like it.

The reporter in the straw hat was at my elbow telling me I had saved the national honor. His full name was Amenophis Rameri Mentuhotep, and he is married to Bet-Anat Sechem, related to the great Septah family. But I called him Straw-hat, as everyone in Cairo did, for he was outstanding in a town where all the natives wore the fez.

He said he wanted to take me on a picnic up the Nile in a *felucca*, one of those mutton-sleeved boats that look so graceful on the postal cards. He had relatives in the village of Sekil, who would, as he said, "give us one bang-up picnic."

I said I had to film the belly dancers on the roof garden

of the New Continental Hotel, but that a picnic would be fine for the morning.

"Egypt is not all belly dancers."

"No, but it's exotic film stuff."

"Tomorrow at nine, and you can bring your director."

"After filming dancers, I can't promise to deliver Mike, but I'll try."

We shook hands on it and he lifted his straw hat off his head in a gesture of see-you-soon, helped by his eyebrows.

EGYPT IN TURMOIL

It would have been better not to be filming stuff in Egypt just then, but the place was in the news and somebody would buy the stuff. Egypt is at the crossroads of its daffy destiny, and makes sense only if you can understand its social and political setups. It's run on a simple, old-fashioned system called graft. A few big families steal everything and exploit for taxes the rest of Egypt. These families are very, very rich. The people are very, very poor.

They suffer from a kind of worm that grows in their filthy river banks (and in their livers) and they are all thin and work hard and suffer and die young, just like the carved coolies slaving away on the stones out in the desert four thousand years old.

The new boss is not a bad guy, everyone says. He'd like to get rid of some of the graft, the crooks, the stealing, but he's trapped by needing the power they control with the wild and savage political parties. Parties who want to wave the green flag of Allah and have a holy war and kill Christians, Jews, and anybody else who gets in their way. This isn't just a pipe dream. The British ("business as usual") have been arming them for years. They have tanks and Spitfire planes, and if, as they hope, the Arab world will rise with its Standard Oil wealth and destroy and destroy, they see hope in a good bloody holy war.

Just how good a fighter the Egyptian is, he didn't prove in the war against the Jews. His officers aren't much, and the graft in supplies goes on. The future of Egypt is anybody's guess. I'm not going to try. The strangest part of it all, here and elsewhere, is that as the British pull out, everyone re-

ON THE NILE

members how kind and good they were for a country. The stealing and despair that follows their withdrawal will yet make them the true heroes of the nineteenth century of Enlightenment.

BELLY-DANCING SISTER ACT

The idea to film the belly dancers of Cairo had been Mike's. It's a native dance form, not very much more daring than our stage dances. The lady comes out veiled, but open

down to her navel (no "falsies" possible of course), and the
dancing is a slow, standing stomp with a little frenzy mixed
up in it. The New Continental had the best dancers, it claimed.
A sister act, two nice brown girls called Katuti and Hekt.

The Continental Roof is a fine place at dusk, with the
Arab rabbis wrapped up for the night on their camel-dung
towers, and the desert wind flapping the awnings. And the
smell of typhoid and typhus from the Nile held down to a
perfumed scent of mud and reeds.

The tables were small, the linen crisp, and the service
courtly. Mike had set up his lights and hidden the camera in
the palm-tree hedge and its brass pots. The music was not
much, but seemed to be a wailed lament plucked on a few
tired strings, and a grinning little boy hitting silver-plated
tin cans from time to time.

"Everything ready, Mike?" I asked him.

"Everything. That Katuti is a honey, but Hekt snaps at
bones for my money. She wants to keep the face veils on."

"It doesn't matter. They all dance veiled."

"But they look like they had no heads."

"I don't think anybody is going to look at their heads."

Mike glanced at me like a sheepdog that had lost his herd.
"I gotta tell you something. To get them to let me take some
footage I had to invite them to the picnic."

I frowned, "That's not honest, Mike. You also promised
them a trip to Hollywood?"

He nodded, "Sure, they're crazy about De Mille pictures."

The tin can-catgut band had started up and the lights had
been dimmed. The curtains parted and "two golden honeys"
(to quote Mike) came slowly out, with thin face veils and little else.

They had bells on their wrists and their legs and a lot of
finger rings. The dance is a courting dance, at least at the
beginning, and then goes into a whirling frenzy, at least it's

KATUTI AND HEKT

a frenzy in Egypt. To Western eyes it's slow and graceful, and rather tied to the ground. The sisters stood still, wriggled their pelves, and made hand gestures that I am sure a professor could explain sixteen ways from home base. It was pretty to watch; the girls were not fat and they knew timing and pace.

Suddenly one of the sisters stopped dancing and hit the other sister in the eye with a pound of charm bracelets and walked off. Hekt, as I found out the one with the black eye was called, let out a howl, called on the gods of Egypt and the cops, and started after her sister with a battle cry. The best part of the dance must have gone on behind the curtain.

Mike came sweating over to me. "Katuti must have been hogging the camera and Hekt must have passed a remark about it."

"Don't say *hog* in a Moslem country, Mike."

"They'll never be civilized here till they get the ham sandwich," Mike said.

"Did you pick up the fight?"

"Oh, sure."

"We'll cut it in as part of the dance."

A FELUCCA ON THE NILE

The girls joined us next day for the boat trip. They were dressed in Fifth Avenue fashions with Paris high-heeled shoes and hairdresses out of something dreamed up in a drug den. They had a few scratches but were friendly again and had their arms around each other and giggled. They had left their face veils at home.

Straw-hat showed up as usual under his hay headgear, and three black grinning boys lugged straw hampers of food.

Straw-hat grinned and rubbed his stomach and winked at the dance act. "Real beer. And *zeytinli prasa*, leeks with olives to nibble on; *hiyar tursus* and *turp*, pickles and radish."

"But the main dish?" asked a sister.

"A pie of pigeons, larks, and chicken with ginger, cardamon seeds, and coconuts shredded." Straw-hat bowed and pinched one of the sisters. "The felucca is ready."

We got aboard. It was a comfortable boat, but had once carried cement. The Nile was the color of a brickyard, and the sail was patched with old flour bags that still read "Gold Medal." We cast off and sailed the Nile, and far off the stone pyramids looked down, eternal and rather snobbish. I sketched, and Mike and Straw-hat made gallant gestures to the dancers. The sun was a hot brass bowl overhead. It was a real pleasant day but warm, and we passed naked little brown men, looking just like the tomb paintings, who drove wet oxen through the mud, pulled a wooden plow as they had been pulling it for four or six thousand years; I was a little rusty on history.

The village of Sekil was neat, green, and goat-tormented. All the relatives of Straw-hat were there to welcome back the boy who had gone to the big city and made good. We were escorted to a fine garden with a fountain in the middle, and the lunch went off very well. Even if the beer had a habit of blowing the neck off the bottle just as you reached to open it.

AT SEKIL

Straw-hat sat on a low chair and shook his head. "To think I came from this mud-hole."

"This looks like a fine place, and the people are fine people."

"But we are backward. We need big things, big ideas."

They say that every place . . .

The trip back to Cairo was a little troubled. The beer had affected the felucca captain and we bounced off a barge full of goats.

TO MAKE A SET

I was sleeping the sleep of the titled the next morning, just hearing the cries of *baksheesh*! from the former kings of Egypt in the streets and the far-off goat calls and the snarl of auto traffic, when the door opened and the dancing sisters came in. I opened one eye and then another, and Katuti stepped forward and said, "We are very sorry, but we can not marry Mike . . ."

I said, "I am happy."

"We promised we would become his wives to get a part in the big cinema you are making here. But we can't."

I wondered what it was all about.

Hekt said, "The truth is we love Amenophis, the one you call Straw-hat. He has two wives already, but a good Moslem is allowed four. We'll complete the set. Mike mustn't take it too hard."

"I'll try and see he's not too hurt."

Katuti said, "We wouldn't have liked America anyway. Mike says the women expose their ears during the day—and that we find indecent. We are sorry."

They left and I went back to sleep.

22   across the sea

WE HAD reached the point where we were working our way home. Any film job that led toward California could get us. We went to Turkey because a New York publisher had cabled me to fly to Istanbul to get color shots of newly uncovered mosaics.

We flew with the *khamsin,* that hot, smothering Egyptian wind, but when we passed over the tight mouth of the Dardanelles and ran up the Sea of Marmora, the *inbat,* the summer breeze of Turkey cooled us, and after hunting the Bosporus in a hot mist, the airfield came up to meet us. We bumped to a landing, and two passport officers went through us quickly but skillfully.

TURKISH AIRFIELD

A trim little man with a high, balding brow and a long cigarette holder came toward me.

"Hajji H. Khalfah, art dealer, at your service," he said,
holding out a yellow-gloved hand to me. "I am to show you
what to film."

I always shake hands with art dealers. "Pleased."

He spoke a mediocre French, and I tried out a halting German. We just about made contact. Sometimes we changed
over and made about the same progress.

"About the paintings?" I began.

"Later, later. How do you like Turkey?"

I said, "It's always changing."

"*Wallahi,* by God, you are right."

We took a taxi over a fairish road that led to the city. The fez and the face veil were long gone, of course, and even the muezzins, who called the hour of prayer, had to wear business suits in public.

I looked at the Byzantine-Ottoman face of Hajji H. Khalfah, and he could have been an art dealer on Fifty-seventh Street, only he looked cleaner and more honest.

"Fine city now."

I agreed. We were passing the busy Galata district with its banks and business houses, and very fancy it looked with the newsboys selling *The Daily Yurt* on the street corners, and businessmen walking around with briefcases as if a merger had just gone off in their hands. The Khalfah Gallery was small, neat, modern, and had two windows. One held two small Guys drawings, and the other a fair copy of the combined schools of Paris, signed Saadeddin.

Inside was a fairy glow of polite, expensive darkness and some soft yellow seats. No pictures.

"Let us go to lunch. My wife would be very happy to meet you. She saw your play, *High Button Slippers,* in Sweden."

I hadn't seen it there myself, and maybe they had changed "shoes" to "slippers." I know little about Sweden.

We got into a small English sports car which Hajji drove as if he were living his last few minutes on earth. He lived in the fashionable Pera district with its new apartment houses, and he said he missed the garden of valonia oak and ilex and the carob trees and fountains. Only the spires of St. Sophia and its dome seemed like old times.

LUNCH IN TURKISH

Mrs. Khalfah, a Circassian, was named Aliye Hanun and was once, I was told (in a proud whisper by her husband) an

actress. It must have been a long time ago. She was an ax-
faced old dame with a sour mouth, tired eyes, and a game way
of putting on her lipstick. She didn't give a *kurush*—penny—
for old-fashioned ways and looked like the lead in a third-rate
road company of *Rain*. But she had very beautiful hands.

"Lunch is just about ready. We shall have American cockballs."

Her husband said softly, "Tails, dear. Tails."

Turkish gin isn't bad, but it shouldn't be used for cockballs.
The table was set with green ceramics, very old, and two old
servants with wisps of palm leaves and peacock tails stood
over us to brush off the summer flies. There were no screens
nor air conditioning. But it was coming, said Hajji. They had
a radio already. "And soon we shall connect it."

Turkish food is not new to me. My mother took me to Turkey when I was five years old and I have been back several
times. I thought of Mama's sad and happy years as we sat down
to lunch. How it brought back the past. The trays of anchovies,
tuna, mullet in brine, slices of smoked sturgeon, and its roe.
Then came the skewered lamb; a fine *dolma*, vine leaves
stuffed with meat; and a rice called *pilaf*; and at last the
eternal sweetmeat, *irmik helvasi*, made of rose-petal flour,
cornmeal, honey, and nuts.

I ate everything and felt very old and very full of the past.
The servants poured rose water over our hands and gave us
the damp towel which has helped so much to spread trachoma
over the Near East.

Hajji smiled and looked at his Swiss wrist watch. "I hope
you will be very pleased as our guest."

ANNA FROM THE PAST

Mrs. Hajji sighed and took two after-dinner pills, and the
art objects on the table rattled. A servant came in like a wide

little tug, towing in the largest woman I had ever seen. She was not only fat, she was huge, big-boned, old, and once very beautiful, I felt sure.

Mrs. Hajji pushed back a flock of tears and said to me, "This is Anna."

The large woman looked at me, leaned over, and kissed my cheek. "Little Stevie."

I was puzzled. The large woman shook her head.

"You don't remember Anna any more?"

"I *am* sorry."

"You've changed, too. The little boy with the blond hair has become a middle-aged man with gray hair. At least, darling, you have kept your hair."

"You're Anna," I said, *"the* Anna."

"I've changed a great deal, too."

Yes, she had. She and Mama had been the gay girls back in 1913. She and Mama had been called the two most beautiful women of their time, and their time was long past. Mama was dead. But there sat Anna cartooned as this tremendous woman, this aging woman looking at me, trying to bring back a past we had once had. The small boy and the beautiful Anna of the soft, white back and the long arms and the red hair and the gleaming, gold-flecked, green eyes. The Anna that Mama paraded with—"for protection." And how Gramp had snorted at that line and swung his cane at the flowers. "For protection! It's the men who need protection! Damn world is going to hell in a hack when two women like you are allowed to run in polite society, and their husbands are off some place making a living for 'em!"

I said, "It's been a long time, Anna."

"Yes, darling, a very old time. And I've shocked you. When Hajji said they were sending a film man from Egypt and said his name was the same as the writer's, I knew it was Sari's boy. We once bought a Renoir in Paris—a Russian

TURKEY-ANNA

paid for it. One of those lousy dukes paid for it. We wanted to buy a Lautrec, but Leo Stein—remember Leo, Stevie? No, I guess you don't—he talked us into the Renoir. Poor Leo is dead, I hear. Whatever happened to that *yenta* of a sister of his?"

"She started a literary movement. She's dead, too. Some people take her very seriously."

"The cow," said Anna.

NIGHT LIFE OF ISTANBUL

It was a very big night. We went to a place called The Golden Horn, which was a French night club with colored jazz and Eurasian girls, and men in evening clothes. For dinner we went to a small place with menus printed in gold leaf. Anna, done up like a battleship in red lead and rustproofing and a green gown that split in the wrong places, was queenly and loud. She puffed on a jade holder and drank wine with a quick gulp and never stopped laughing.

"Stevie, darling, there's life in the old gal yet. Lots of life. Sari would be proud of you, taking an old lady around the night spots. This place used to be wonderful. German and British Embassy boys, and rich Russians who had *mujika* to flog. What fine beasts the Russians were in those days. Wolf collars and black eyebrows and little white teeth, and such vodka and caviar! Not just black caviar, but the big, fat, gray stuff, too. Drink from a lady's slipper, my eye. Those boys used to . . ."

The next morning was rather grim. I felt the futility of human endeavor, and there was little top to my head. I put the head under cold water and, with what was left of my mind, I worried over Mike, out filming the stuff we had come for.

The taxi took me to a shabby row of flats overlooking a line of decaying trees. Anna had a red door and a small room furnished with darkness and tattered wallpaper; it smelled of spilled *raki*.

She was sitting in a deep chair looking up at a drawing of Mama as a Gibson Girl. She held a sticky glass of *raki* and looked at me and smiled.

"Hung over?"

"Like a mountain climber, Anna."

She grinned and refilled the glass. "It doesn't matter, darling. I'm old and falling apart. I can't last much longer. I'll get by. They can't count the old girl out just yet. It isn't much of a world any more, Stevie. They've taken the color out of it and made it damn dull. It isn't the golden times or weather of what it once was, and will never be again. The world has lost more than its values and its sense of humor; it has lost its desire to live fully and let the next man alone. We had a motto in the old days—if you don't like it, don't knock it—but now they're prying apart the atom and making their plows over into flying bombs. I must really feel bad to talk like this. Kiss me, Stevie, and go away. It's been good seeing you, and now I can finish off the few dance steps left to me on this mortal coil and go and see what Sari is doing some place else . . . Pass the bottle, darling."

I left her there and I felt tired in the sunlight. I decided the sooner I got home, the better. While we waited I filled my sketchbook with a lot of things . . .

THE TROUBLE SHOOTER

The American trouble shooter for the oil company was a neat, blond young man, ten years out of Yale, five years away from a war plant, and just back from the hellholes of Arab oil fields. We had our drinks in the cool inside of the café, and the flies buzzed on the sticky paper on the ceiling, dying slowly in the smell of damp sugar, spilt rum, and old rugs.

"We Americans—what do we know and what can we do? Sometimes it's dark, and sometimes it's like stopping the sea from having a tide."

"Does it boil down to anything?" I asked.

"Only one lug's opinion, but based on what I've seen in the last two years, *if* you want it."

"I want it," I said, cooling my hands around the drink.

"The U.S. policy is good, but it's not tough enough. It's got to get mean and tough. Some of our Congressmen lost us India for a long time by holding up surplus wheat to starving millions. We're too good to the Arabs because they have the oil. We can't trust them in a war. They'll welcome the Russians if the Russians put a lot of cash, gold, on the line. We ought to arm Israel to the teeth to hold the Middle East with the Turks for us, if they have to."

"What about the Reds in Asia?"

"Maybe we can hold them back. But they've real native revolts against white landowners. We've got to win them back, not by arms and tanks but by beating the Reds to the job of dividing the land. Chiang Kai-shek is a dead duck—forget him. He's stolen billions and his family and relatives are investing it in the stock market in the U.S.A. He can't put any real, young, trained soldiers on our side. We can't trust him. And the Philippines? Democracy kind of upset them . . . gave them a bellyache. We should stick to them but should force them to tame the Huks by giving them real land and by getting the crooks out of the government. They can work it if we give them honest men."

"We can't. It's up to them. They elect whom they want."

"Don't make me laugh. In Asia we must have peace and order. And we must do it with the right people. No playboys, fat old China hands, no obsolete regimes. And real fundamental reform. Forget democracy as a vote, and make it food and land and freedom. Old social patterns have to go, feudal bosses and systems. Otherwise, the people will just sit back and let the Reds come in."

"What about our loans and gifts?"

"No good. The big boys steal them. We've got to invent a way to get the stuff to the people direct. Don't ask me how. And this race business. We can't go on calling them gooks, shines, chinks, greasespots, geeks, boys, and hey. The Reds are moving fast. We can't build a Great Wall like the Ch'in emperors did. And we can't depend on the few rice Christians our missions made in Asia. Let's face it, they have faiths so much older than ours that we're never going to make a dent in their own godheads."

"You feel any hope?" I said.

ARAB OIL

"When I see the Abadan refineries closed down in Iran I see what softheads we are. We should have forced the issue there. Our common effort should be to save each other."

"That's pushing people around."

"It's not the people any place—it's one or two guys and his pals. How about another drink?"

"Sure. You feel we're doing it wrong but can do it right?"

He said, "We have to do something. Spending isn't enough. It needs long-time planning, but I'm an engineer—I think that way."

"In what way do we understand Asia least?" I asked.

"Not just in not admitting political imperialism and economic imperialism are washed up, but that Asia dislikes our disregard of their old cultures. Cultures thousands of years older than ours. We lack respect for their spiritual ideas. General MacArthur made no friends by suggesting the Christianization of Japan."

"We're getting around to letting other peoples' gods alone."

"The power of the Prophet Mohammed rules the near Middle East . . . Arabian, Turkish, and Persian is the Islamic text from Morocco to Indonesia, to the Philippines. And the Far East is the home and sacred ground of Taoism, Confucianism, and Buddhism. But does any Sunday school class in Kansas respect this?"

"It's a problem," I admitted, "trying to export freedom of religion."

"So there it is, all mixed and scowling, each at the other. Western Nationalism, Islamic Asia, and the wolf peoples' Soviet Marxism. And we don't admit that old cultures and altars, these ancient civilizations, are having a great resurgence. The law of the Koran, the wisdom of the Chinese Gent, the grave of the Buddha-head are as important as the Gospel, the Song of Songs, and the Last Judgment."

"Who's going to win?" I asked.

"Who knows? The side that makes the least mistakes. But our State Department and the Vatican and the U.N. make the error of thinking there is only one truly Semitic religion. Well, there are three: Judaism, Christianity, and Mohammedanism. All have their unique revelations. It's a hassel. A real hassel."

"You think faiths will decide, not arms?"

"Don't ask an engineer that. He only does the plans. People put up the projects."

book 4

THE SOUND OF
BLOODY LAUGHTER

IN INDIA—FREE SOUP

23   peace in Pakistan

MIKE and I were still heading east. We did a lot of filming of the usual stuff.

"Pakistan-Makistan isn't much fun any more," Hattie, the
lady reporter, said to me as we broiled in the sun waiting for
a taxi at the Lahore Airport. "It used to be a real-class joint.
The Paris of India. British brass, Chinese millionaires, and
fancy boys and girls from the best black-sheep families. But
then nothing is like it used to be, is it? The posh hotels in
Peshawar, Rawalpindi, are run down. All you get to feed the
face is goat, and likker now comes only on an official permit."

The place looked bad. The burned houses of the great riots of 1947 had been pulled down and the buzzards had finished off the dead long ago. It looked like a frontier town in a bad movie. Mike came over, lugging his heavy camera. "What we waitin' for? There ain't goin' to be no red rug out for us."

"A hotel taxi," said Hattie, taking off her fur jacket in the heat of the day. "The Faletti used to be the best hotel. They cook chicken twenty-two different ways. Good curries, too."

Mike looked over the mob of natives, sunbathing standing up, their white *Jinnah* caps shining. "What kind of a newsreel shot is it?"

Pakistan was involved in some important border and partition meeting. The whole of India had been carved up fast when the British called it a jolly good day in 1947. Half a million people had been killed since. There was rumor of more trouble in Iran and Afghanistan, and someone in London had thought it would be good newsreel material.

We had been promised some shots of Liaquat Ali Khan, the Prime Minister. But I was wondering if it was worth the trip to the capital, at Karachi.

The taxi came . . . and we went up to the Faletti Hotel and got rooms. Hattie said the place was run down. "The British give tone to a place. Here everything is to show how little they care for the past."

Two fat men passed, their tobacco-brown faces wrapped in long mustaches.

Hattie nodded. "Rulers from Bahawalpur and Khairpur. They've all become part of Pakistan. They bow to the *Wali-ahad* and take cash on the barrel."

Mike asked, "What's a *Wali-ahad*?"

"The heir apparent," said Hattie. "Let's get some stingahs and food inside us."

"Great idea," said Mike.

NATIVE HOTEL LIFE

It was very hot and the air conditioning worked at rare moments. In the streets the flies buzzed and camel carts went past, their balloon tires stolen from American air dumps long since swallowed up by jungle. A fancy mosque hung in the violet light of the noon heat and even the dogs had gone off to hunt shade.

The dining room was cool, but rather empty. Two pale men from the Security Council of the U.N. still trying to settle the Kashmir business in which two hundred and fifty thousand of the population had died in riots. A Moslem Pathan with scar

PAKISTAN CITIZEN

tissue on his face sat scowling at us, and a fat Turk, who ate a great deal, smiled several gold-front teeth at everyone.

During the war Hattie had been famous as a reporter. She claimed she spent week ends in Moscow with Stalin and knew Churchill from the cigar down, and it seemed the invasion plans were partly *her* idea. At least that's how it seemed in her books, as she told it. She was a very good, very beautiful reporter and it wasn't her fault that wars were cold these days and gal reporters hard up for excitement.

Hattie had been here twice before and she ordered for us. She waved off the bill of fare the native boy held out to us. "Never order what's on the bill of fare. It's been around a long time and tired. Let's have *kharoof mahshy*. They do it well here."

Mike said, "Sounds like goat to me."

Hattie grinned, "It's roast stuffed kid and very good. The three of us should do away with the little chap." Hattie was rather British at the moment, but she didn't call lunch tiffin, or chop, the way they do in the movies.

It was some lunch. Two big, strong boys came in with a pan two yards across. It was the size of a small bridge table. A wall of well-cooked rice went around the pan, held up by slices of hard Arab bread. Several whole chickens and vegetables swam in the middle of the pan. It smelled of marjoram and mint, of paprika and cinnamon powder.

Plates were set before us, but *no* spoons or forks.

Hattie grinned. "I ordered this native style. Watch little Hattie tuck in."

We watched. Very skillfully, she put her hand into the pan. She picked up a bit of chicken, rolled a rice blanket on it, and popped the ball into her mouth.

"With the fingers?" Mike asked.

"That's right. Little rice balls, a little chicken. Come on in, the gravy's fine."

HATTIE, THE GLAMOUR GAL

It took a little courage, but soon we were up to our wrists in food. It takes a bit of doing. One uses the fingers and the thumb, and after a while it seems very normal.

We had an official permit for our health to drink wine; and they served a *khmer* made, it seemed to me, of dates, but strong enough to please anyone. Moslems do not drink in public, but they break the laws of the Koran in private, just like everyone else.

The lunch took a long time and the streets still burned with heat as we finished. Hattie went up to her room to knock out her copy for her newspapers, which she did very quickly. Mike hired a car and went to shoot food markets and saddle shops on film. I went to bed and pulled the insect nets around me and had an hour of good sleep.

THE GREAT SHOE MYSTERY

I was awakened by a knock on the door and Hattie came in—fully dressed but barefooted. "Somebody stole my shoes!"

I got up and yawned. "Haven't you any other pair?"

"I *had* three pairs. They're gone too! While I was taking a bath."

Hattie has small, beautiful feet and she wears very fine shoes of rare pelts and fancy finishing.

"Well, I guess some poor gal couldn't resist your fancy stuff. Better order up some native slippers."

"It's a good thing they don't like nylons or I'd be as naked as a jaybird at a crows' picnic. Well, get dressed, we're invited to dinner at the cotton king's palace."

"I'm here to shoot some newsreel stuff. Very fine stuff, cotton, but not exciting."

Mike came in carrying a heavy-mounted saddle. Mike collects saddles and it's a habit worse than first editions or stamps, because saddles take up space.

"Not *another* saddle?"

Mike grinned. "Don't worry, character, I didn't have to pay for it. The guy that owns the saddle shop is marrying off his daughter tonight. I'm going to film it for him."

"We're here to film world-shaking subjects. Take it back."

Hattie shook her head and rubbed a nude toe. "No. You never give back anything that a Moslem gives you. Big insult. Much bloodshed. You warp his honor. Catch on?"

"The saddle stays," I said as Mike put it down on the bed.

"It's going to be a fine wedding."

"I'm not going to any wedding, or any cocktail party by a cotton king."

Of course I went to both since the only cinema palace in town was running an old picture of mine, *Stallion Road*—an epic of which the motion picture critic of *The New Yorker* had once said (quote): "If you're a horse you'll like this picture . . ."

The palace of the cotton king was guarded by armed Pathans. It seemed that just a few months ago a lot of Hindu fanatics, the Dogra tribes from the foothills of the Himalayas, had infiltrated into town and cut off a few heads. Politics is a mean business here. India isn't a healthy place when the fireworks start. Up the Kohat Pass, at Dera Adamkhel, the Moslems have their arms center where native blacksmiths make modern arms, and as soon as they have a lot more, the host told me, they were "going to rake over India."

The host was a very dark man with a beard scented with sandalwood and jeweled hands with long nails. There were no women at the party, except Hattie. Moslems still keep their women locked up.

We sat on low stools and drank sherbets and the host said the income tax was killing him.

"You and me both," said Mike, "but you ain't got the alimony troubles I got."

The host smiled, "I have fifty-two ex-wives. And I support them all."

"You win," said Mike. "When are the dancing girls coming on?"

The host shook his head. "I don't keep slave girls in town. Only in my country place. It takes years to develop a dancing girl. Like good wine, which I am forbidden to drink. I can't trust them in town. People steal them."

"And no insurance I suppose," said Mike, let down. He also collected dancing girls. That and saddles.

The host clapped his hands. "I have some singers. Four girls. You will like them. They will sing an old favorite of mine."

Four fat girls came out—very plain of face—their heavy harem pants ending in tight silver bracelets. They swayed and began to sing shrill, ear-banging music.

Hattie was looking at the feet of the singers. They all wore high-heeled modern shoes. Hattie got up and lifted the leg of one of the singers, like a blacksmith inspecting a hoof. She went down the line examining every high heel.

I said to the host, "Reporters, you know, do strange things. Most likely going to write a story on the feet of your dancing —pardon me, singing girls."

"Ah, *you* Americans," said the host.

Hattie came back and sat down. I looked at her and she shook her head. "No . . . cheap Jap models copying Paris. Not mine."

We left soon after that. The singers had reached their version of an old Arab love chant.

LOCAL WEDDING

The wedding was in the slum section of the town and was proper ritual, and full of smoke. The women were hidden from view by a curtain, but we could hear them chattering like birdseed eaters. The bridegroom was dressed in red and sat alone while the bride, hidden in drapes and face cloths and weighted down with pounds of gold coin, sat facing him. A Moslem rabbi was tying their sashes together, and a band made sounds that were nearly music.

The father of the bride, smelling of the best saddles, greeted us and gave us hard bread and salt which we ate and then we sat down on the floor and a huge pan came in, followed by

a dozen more. The saddle-maker was going "the whole hog,"
Mike said, but we hissed him silent. One doesn't say "hog"
in Moslem circles.

The best food, I was told, was *baby camel Kharoof,* which
is made just like the roast stuffed kid, only they use a baby
camel, the way we use baby lamb. It looked rather sinister
and was served with *teen makoud,* a fig conserve.

AT THE WEDDING

The saddle-maker insisted we try the baby camel, and Mike
and I looked at each other, trapped. It was just fair.

I am happy to say the baby camel was soon gone—the poor
relatives had gobbled it up, and they sat now with happy, oily
mouths smiling up at us, and we said it was all right, we would
take the rice *pilaf* and the Turkish *shish kebab* which was
coming in on flaming swords.

Hattie never did get her shoes back, but she did get a jacket
made of baby tiger.

INDIA ON ITS OWN

Mike and I went on into India proper. Hattie went north to see a rajah who raised fighting elephants, which seemed an old-fashioned idea, like building covered wagons.

India was very big and very crowded. Some of it made a little sense to me, but the country and its problems are too big for one visiting mind—for mine, anyway.

I was raised on books about India like *Kim, Soldiers Three, King of the Khyber Rifles,* and *The Moonstone.* I've had a hard time adjusting to the facts. India is complex, bedeviling, and I don't understand much of it. The little I know, and what I have seen, is not much help. Jawaharlal Nehru is a good man and honorable, but just how good he is for India and how much of a fighter he is in a world of wolf teeth, time will show. His Congress party is controlled mostly by the cotton kings, the big-business boys, and they worry more over their bank-rolls than about Reds, famines, and poverty.

India is full of hatred. The Hindus for the Sikhs, the Brahmins for the non-Brahmins. The land is packed with madmen, priests, and princes—all snarling and playing off ideas and forces against one another. And the people starve. Not just as figures of speech. Their ribs stick out, they drop dead in the street in front of you, they drag themselves with their begging bowls from door to door. Holy cows and monkeys roam by the millions and no one dares touch them as they eat anything within their reach. Caste, superstition, and greed are kings in India. Disease is their daily bread and squabbling and nepotism are the rules of office and power.

I'm tired of writing of stealing in high places all over the world. It must have existed before, but at least there once seemed enough for all to steal. Now there is danger that one more crook in power will tip the scales into the fire. The Communists, the holy men, the Moslem cutthroats, the black-market boys, wait to play their own hand when their turn comes up. The problems of sickness, poverty, and famine don't approach any real settlement.

LAHORE—PARIS OF INDIA

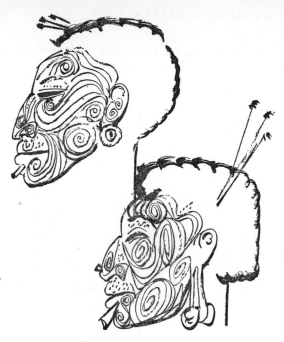

ISLAND DIVERS FOR MOONSTONES

24   Polynesians are people

IF YOU like life beyond sin and calories, the place to go is the group of islands known as the Polynesian group. They may not be all the travel posters say, but they are wonderful for freedom.

Mike Murd and I got to an island called Monox Four one lazy afternoon, bent on shooting some pearl divers. As our journey drew to an end and trouble boiled over in Asia, we felt a little better about getting home.

Monox Four was a company island, part of a group owned by a soap company that bought up its coconuts and kept the natives in comic books, recordings of *South Pacific*, and hair

ribbons worn by both sexes. Mike looked over the island and
shook his head.

"We build them better in Hollywood."

"You mean it looks faked?"

"Sure, the back lot at Metro has a better native village.
Look at those roofs, tin roofs made from signs reading,
'Standard Oil.' "

MONOX FOUR, AN ISLAND

"It does keep out the rain."

"And jeeps! Holy cow, imagine jeeps on a South Sea
island."

"There used to be a war around here."

"I still don't like it."

Mike, under his bark, was a romantic. I have no use for
romantics any more. Maybe because I used to be a romantic
myself. I got rid of that dreamy outlook on men, morals, and
women. There was enough shock around to make me want to

see life without the rose-colored glasses. I liked the tin roofs, and the jeep was handy to take us up to Ali's place, a sort of trading post run by a half-Irish, half-Arab gentleman called, of course, Ali. We had a letter of introduction to him, and he stopped sorting some moonstones to smile at us.

"Bad season for camera work."

"Can we see some diving?"

"All the time. Care to buy some moonstones?"

"Maybe later."

"I'll throw in a free set of recordings of *South Pacific*. By the original cast."

"No, thanks."

"I'm stuck with a hundred sets. At first the natives were amused by the stuff, but now I can't move them."

"Too bad," said Mike, "civilization is the curse of the tropics. Only it's not gin and clothing any more, it's films and records."

Ali put away his collection of moonstones. "Things were simple in the old days, my old man used to tell me. The missionaries used to land with Bibles, and the natives had the land. In a few years the natives had the Bibles, and the missionaries had the land. A man could make a decent buck in those days. How would you fellas like to go to big party?"

Mike beamed, "You mean one with native rituals and stuff?"

Ali shook his head. "The headman just got a new Buick and he's celebrating. He put his name down in 1949 and it just came through."

"That's better than you do in Beverly Hills," I said.

PARTY IN A GROVE

The party was held in a big grove of coconut trees, and the car was covered with flowers. The headman made us welcome and introduced us to his daughter, who was a real native type in her California sun hat and Hollywood sun glasses. But the food, at any rate, was the real thing. We sat on the ground and thanked the Lord we still could eat in Polynesia.

The food was wrapped in banana and taro and breadfruit leaves and cooked in great pits filled with hot stones. They grated taros and yams and soaked them in coconut milk. The fish, freshly caught and still colored like the rainbow, were packed in huge banana leaves and baked between flat stones heated as hot as they could get. Prawns, crayfish, everything was wrapped and cooked.

The pig was the best of it. It was the headman's own pig, and he was rather proud of it.

The natives had learned to drink American soda and beer, but for those who could take it there was the native kava, made from the fibers of the kava, fermented with some *fo* plants that give it a licorice flavor. I didn't care for it, but Mike seemed to think it was pretty good.

After the food, we went up to the headman and asked if we could film the boys diving.

"Sure," said the headman, "but we dive for moonstones."

"No sponge- or pearl-diving?" Mike asked.

"No money in those any more. But moonstones, pretty fair. I want to save up and go to America."

"We're going home ourselves," Mike said.

"Good deal. You see *South Pacific*?"

We admitted we hadn't. The headman seemed shocked. "How come?"

"Never got around to it," I said.

"Too bad. One thing I want to do, see that *South Pacific*."

"But you live in the South Pacific . . . why worry about a show that isn't very real?" Mike asked.

"Here," the headman said, "the women they get fat, here is always taxes and trouble and the boys wrecking the jeeps

THE HEADMAN'S PARTY

and the banana trees dying. In play, all the women are beautiful, they sing much better than our girls, and the music has
more beat. Do you get me?"

"I get you, Jackson," Mike said, "but it's all made up."

"The people on the stage are real, no?"

"They are, yes," I said. "We'll film the divers in the morning and hope the clouds look good."

We went back to Ali's where we had rented his second-best
room. Mike took off his shoes and drank some old army beer.

"How do you like these cookies? They have everything, and
they want to see a show about a place you could never find on
a map."

"They're romantic, Mike, like you."

"Is that a dirty word?"

"It's a state of mind, Mike, in which everything is twice lifesize and everybody is beautiful."

"Is that bad?"

I pulled the insect net tight around as I got into bed. "You walk around starry-eyed and then somebody hits you over the head with the biggest club in the world and you wake up counting your illusions on the floor. Resign from the romantics. The headman had better, or they'll take back his Buick."

Mike looked at me and shook his head, "I think the quicker we get you home, the better. You'll be attackin' love next, and this I ain't goin' to stand."

"Take a nap, Mike; beer catches up with you in the tropics."

"Yeah . . . you know, this ain't at all like the movies we used to make."

"Nothing is ever like the movies, Mike."

I heard a snore. Mike was sleeping on his back, his mouth open, some empty beer cans around him.

MOONSTONE DIVING

It rained that night, several hundred times. It would come down on the tin roof making thunder and fury, then it would stop and a dripping effect would take over for some time. Then it would get hot under the roof, and the insects would try to find the lamp to light it and play games, and then the rain would start again. It was that way until morning. Mike slept through all and woke up with the sunlight bathing his battered features.

We went out to the diving grounds and found a lot of handsome men with big, brown bodies going off small boats into fifty feet of water. The water was very clear, and we could take pictures right to the bottom. Little fish fed bigger fish, and the coral growths on the bottom looked like a pretty garden in a New England village. We took a lot of footage of the moonstone divers and went up to have lunch with the headman.

His daughter was wearing Paris slacks and reading a novel by Evelyn Waugh. It turned out she had gone to college in California and hoped Papa would make enough money some day so she could live in Pasadena and ride in the horse shows. She was a very bright girl and couldn't do the native dances or sing the native songs. I could see Mike felt very let down about this, because he always expected life to be just like the movies he used to direct.

It rained while we were at lunch, and it leaked.

The headman looked up and shook his head. "Since the Army left, it's pretty hard to get Standard Oil cans."

His daughter grinned. "That's the trouble with a civilized war. They build you up to expect solid comforts like Kleenex and canned pork and beans and cold cream and girdles, and then they finish their old war and leave us here to go back to banana-leaf underwear and fish bones in our hair."

The headman shook his head. "Just because you've been educated, don't mock our ways."

We spent the evening listening to Ali play his record collection and lament his stock of Rodgers and Hammerstein.

In the morning we were back at the diving ground, and Mike got the idea of going down in an old diving suit left on the island and letting me take pictures of him spearing fish.

I didn't like the looks of the diving suit, but Mike was game, and as I was happy not to be asked to take the dive, I agreed.

We got Mike into the patched canvas suit and explained to the boys how to keep the air pump going. Mike opened the little glass window in the battered brass head of the suit.

"Let's get the signals right. One pull, okay. Two pulls, more air. Three pulls hard, get me the hell *up*."

"Understand?" I said to the native who owned the suit.

"Sure, kid."

Mike asked, "What's two pulls?"

"Ding dong," said the native.

"The trolley song," said Mike. "No, two pulls means more air. Got it?"

"Free air, you said it, boy," said the native.

I asked, "Where did you learn English?"

"P. G. Wodehouse book, headman's daughter she lend him, hot stuff, oh you kid."

"You bet," said Mike. "Keep an eye on me, character. I have an idea this lug thinks human life is some lark."

MIKE UNDER THE SEA

Mike closed his little window, the air bubbled in and out, and he sank slowly, a fish spear in his hand. It took him a long time to reach bottom, then he waved and did a slow walk, like a ballet step, and lunged at a fish. He missed, and the natives laughed, and I had to poke them to get them pumping air again.

A big fish passed; Mike sideswiped it, and it pulled him off his feet. He took a head-over-heels fall, very slow, and went over and over.

When he got up again, I could see him gesturing with a closed fist and stamping around, but the fish and spear were gone for good.

I gave the signal to pull him in, and he came up slowly— I didn't want a case of bends on my hands. We got Mike's little window open in the brass head. He had turned a nice shade of blue and was breathing hard. The suit had leaked and water was dripping over his face.

"How'd I do?" he asked.

"Well, we didn't get any shots of you spearing a fish."

"Did you see the one that got away? Musta been twenty feet long."

The native who owned the suit shook his head. "Three feet most like, maybe."

"Pulled like a wild bull."

"You owe ten dollars for spear."

"Ten bucks!"

"Sure, that no native spear. I order him from Sears-Roebuck . . . Steel shaft, tempered head. Best."

Mike scowled. "You can say what you want, but there ain't no simple children of nature, and maybe never was. Ten bucks!"

"Ten dollars," the native repeated.

We got to Ali's, and he said a steamer was standing off the next island and would pick us up, the radio had said, *if* we got there before morning.

"How do we get there?"

"The headman has a motorboat . . . he can do it."

We went to see the headman, and he said he was sorry. He had a motorboat but only three tins of gas, the real old Standard Oil tins, and he wasn't going to use it up for nonsense.

"When does the next boat stop here?" I asked.

"Oh, maybe in two weeks."

"We want to go, we've been away a long time. We'll pay double."

"What good is money? It can't replace the gas."

Mike rubbed his red face and smiled. "Look, you want an autographed picture of Pinza, of *South Pacific*?"

"So?"

"You get us to that ship. And we send you a personal picture, signed by Pinza, saying: 'To my friend, headman of Monox Four, with love and admiration, Ezio Pinza'—or however he signs it."

"Well?"

THE DAUGHTER OF THE CHIEF

"And with the tin cans you can fix the roof. It's not neat to eat off a wet table."

That did it. We got to the steamer just as she was getting ready to pull out and we waved to the headman and his daughter and promised to send her a year's supply of *Vogue*.

We stood at the rail, the hot wind drying us off, and as the motorboat went spanking off across the sea, Mike shook his head.

"I think I'm resigning from the romantics club, too. Nothing was right on that island. I've made a dozen South Sea pictures, and I know the real McCoy. *That* wasn't it."

I left Mike at the rail, still talking.

25   Hawaii is still an island

TO A lot of travelers, the Hawaii Archipelago is a string of wonderful pearls—Kauai and Maui, and Hawaii itself. But the best of all is on the island of Oahu, where sits the city of Honolulu above the Kaiwi Channel, looking just like the colored newsreel shots of it. I went below and awakened Mike and we came on deck, the morning gin-and-lime in our stomachs. Leaning on the rail, we enjoyed the sights.

"Nothing like it," said Mike, trying to come fully awake.

"You're not a *malihini*?" I asked.

"Who you calling a greenhorn? I been here six times to make pictures. I can smell a *luau* cooking from here."

The dock was a busy sight of people coming, and people

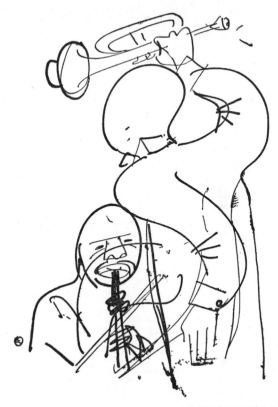

AT THE HOTEL LUAU

going, and people *just* watching. And there just watching was a tall, excited woman, and she smiled and said, "I'll be a cockeyed pineapple! Look who's here!"

"Miss Tone," I said. "My director, Mike Murd."

"Hello," said Mike. "How's the island?"

"Filthy hot, filthy fun. Good to see old drinking friends."

"Here long?" I asked.

"Avoiding my fourth husband," she said. "A week . . . taking tourist boat shots for a company."

This called for a drink and we went up to the hotel to have it.

There was a big *luau* back of the hotel that night and Miss Tone fell into the *poi* bowl. *Poi* is the fermented pink paste of the grated taro plant—but I never cared for it. It's eaten with a finger; one dips and sucks and makes faces. The best thing there was *na papai hoopihapiha,* or filled crabs. The crabs are steamed in boiling water, the meat is picked out and sautéed with garlic, onions, tomatoes, and lime juice.

It was a good place to rest.

The smart journalists call the Territory of Hawaii a brown-and-white mosaic, but that's just being fancy. It's real and alive and stirring in the sun. And the hula dancers, ukulele players, and Vandyke-colored beach and surf-board bums are pretty phony. But the island bosses, called The Big Five Companies, are very real. The offices of the sugar and pine-apple barons between Bishop and Fort streets are busy and air conditioned, and geared to big business and big payoffs through their powerful lobbies in Washington.

THE BOSSES

"Hell, if these gooks ever become a state and have state's rights, we're dead," one of the managers told me over a tall, very cold Tom Collins. "Sugar and the Matson Steamship Line own this place, and you can't make real Americans out of these colored people. They'd turn Red and make Harry Bridges head man. The sonofabitch has unionized almost everything out here anyway, except a ten-dollar lay in Madame Liu's place. And the Chinks are moving into Waikiki beach houses so fast, you'd think we minded sending our laundry downtown."

"You from the South?" I asked.

"Yeah. South Boston."

The other side to the picture is confusing but exciting. Japanese, Hawaiian, Filipino, Puerto Rican, and a lot of just

Anglo-Saxon and Irish half-breeds. They live the best they can, have lots of laughs and lots of troubles. There is still Buddhist culture, and Shinto shrines, and a few kimonos and *geta*. But, mostly, it's jazz and hot rods and movie fans and eaters of hot dogs and drinkers of cokes, just as in West Hernia, Texas, or even Philadelphia.

THE NATIVE

A rising young taxi driver with three cabs explained it to me in his college English.

"Let's face it—we breeds are part of a semi-colonial economic culture. The Reds give us a pain in the ass and we hate

CITIZENS OF MIXED BREEDS

the big shots that came here as missionaries four generations ago and took over the coffee and pineapples and Macadamia nuts and orchids. I'm half-Chinese and part Filipino; my wife, she's Hawaiian, Swede, and Malay. The kids are cute, but you can't figure them. Take a look. I always carry their pictures."

They were very beautiful children, and I said so.

"I'm going to send the boy to Stanford, and the girls to Mills. I want them to be somebody. I'm getting four more cabs. They can't push me around."

"How was it during the war?"

"Christ, they gave you a shovel and said, dig in. Only I was in the Army, under Dugout Doug."

"Who?"

"That · · · · · · MacArthur. He grandstanded us into a Jap prison camp for three years. But I'm not beefing. I'm getting along. My old man could never speak English, and my old lady never took off the native outfit. I like democracy, what part they let me have. And the tourists keep coming."

"What would you advise people to see out here?"

"The colors of the Kauai Waimea canyon, the Crater of the Sun up on Haleakala on Maui, and the black sand beaches on the big island itself."

"How about the pineapples?"

"Mister, we hate pineapples."

"Why?"

"They brought a lot of greed and pushing around to the islands. It was all right before they canned them, but now it's big politics."

THE LAST ROMANTIC

I sat in the garden making notes. A big party was on. Everyone was getting high.

Miss Tone came over to where we were sitting.

"Have you ever thought of getting married?" she asked Mike.

"Too many times."

"I'm a lousy romantic," Miss Tone said. "I'm just romantic in every pore, that's my trouble. I like all men and I cry a lot about it later, but you can't keep a romantic gal down."

"That's the character," said Mike.

I took her up to her hotel and got the hotel clerk's wife to put her to bed. I was reading when Mike came in and sat down and took off one shoe and looked at it.

"You know that old gal is right . . . it's a romantic place."

"She's an old dear friend of mine, she's not old."

"Sorry. Maybe it's the moonlight, or the surf on the shore, or the way the roads wind up to the pineapples, but I feel like a young calf in a green field. Hell, there I go getting full of moonlight and roses. When do we get home?"

"As soon as we get some money wired us for the films we shipped. It costs money to live in all this moonlight."

Mike decided to sleep on the idea of money, and I rolled over and woke up with the phone ringing in my ear. It was Miss Tone.

"Hello, rise and shine. It's Baby."

"What time is it, dawn?"

"You didn't come here to sleep, did you? There's a party at a fruit farm a friend of mine runs. I'm bringing you."

"Do I have to go? We're getting older."

"Pick you up in half an hour."

She did too . . .

"How do I look?" she said, spinning around.

"Greatest show on earth," I said. "But why silver nail polish?"

"My fortuneteller said it would bring luck."

"You still go to soothsayers?"

"They control my life. I used to be unhappy when I thought for myself. Now they just tell me what to do. Don't I look happy?"

"Gibberingly," I said, and we all piled in with the other guests into small cars driven by wild men in beach shirts.

Oahu, like all the islands of the Archipelago, is beautiful. The sun shines, the black mountains are against the skies, little clouds puff along like wool brushings. Then suddenly the rains. A green downpour, a great wetting of earth and leaf. Just as suddenly it is over and the rainbows cross your path and *drip, drip,* is every place. Then the sun again, lime-white and powerful, the shadows blue and delicate violet and

NATIVE GIRL (IRISH-CHINESE-HUNGARIAN)

the fields green and the plants growing. On the mountains the mist lingers a few minutes, then it, too, is gone and the dark teeth of mountains are up there again. Everything grows here and grows with lush ease. We passed guavas, custard apples, pomegranates, mangoes, the aromatic carambola, oranges, lemons, limes, the dark, surly avocados, the cigar-shaped tamarind, and *all* the pineapples in the world.

Miss Tone's friend was a little man with a pot belly and a long cigar and a lot of servants all over the place, and before we knew it, the party had started. People came and people went, and the host served everybody and smiled.

He was a nice little man and he gave me a cigar and got me into a corner.

"I wish this party would end. It's been going on for five days."

"Oh, I thought it just started."

"No. Miss Tone started it, but I can't stop it."

I grinned. "Great girl."

The little man went off to see if everybody was trying the rum drinks. It had rained again, and the sky was crayon-blue, and the pink foothills under the purple mountain range were more beautiful than anything I had even seen. The native girls, an army of sensual service, were bringing in more food. I latched onto a platter of pickled salmon called *lomi lomi*. This was followed by a vegetable soup flavored with pineapple; *kupa hala ai me kahi meaai lunanhelehele*, and baked lobsters; not just baked but toasted on hot stones buried underground.

I found Mike in a corner eating oyster fritters with two native girls. "Having fun?" he asked me.

"I'm doing all right."

One of the native girls giggled. "Mr. Wald is promising us jobs in his next picture."

Mike grinned and swallowed an oyster. I looked at my

wrist watch. "Look, Jerry," I said to Mike, "don't you think you better go back to worrying over your productions for next year?"

"Aw, we'll miss the *I'a malao*."

"We will?"

One of the native girls nodded. "We promised Mr. Wald a special order of Bombay duck and dried salt fish."

"He'd better come . . . duck never agrees with him."

"Oh, this is hung in feathers for two years, over the door."

Mike had a sip of *hala ai wai* and got up. "Maybe I better see how Howard Hughes is doing while I'm gone."

Outside, the host was watching some people getting into the cars. He said to me, "Come back any time."

"We're leaving in a few days."

"Too bad," he suddenly brightened and shook hands on it.

Mike was very still all the way back to the hotel. We didn't see Miss Tone for two days. She was supposed to sail with us.

SHIP AT SEA

We got our money and space on the boat . . . our cabin looked like a war hoarder's delight. Sides of ham, a whole suckling pig in aspic, a keg of island rum, and more fruit than the Lord could ever afford in Eden.

I didn't see Miss Tone at dinner so I went below and found her cabin. I knocked and I was told to come in. She was seated at a dressing table arranging a daring evening gown on her figure.

"We'll have dinner in a moment."

"Dinner is over," I said.

"Odd. I must have slept through it. Well, let's go up on deck and show the passengers a treat."

We sat in deck chairs.

"It's time I changed my type."

"Care for a drink?"

"I'm not drunk. I'm just remembering what you once told me about Proust. 'You haven't lived anything you can't remember.'"

MARKET

26   they eat a lot in Costa Rica

MIKE got a radiogram from Hollywood, a rush call. He
would leave us at the first port and take a plane north. I was
sorry he was going. He was a solid, hard-boiled person, very
comforting.

The night we sighted the coast of Costa Rica and went up
the smooth waters of Coronada Bay, we gave a masked ball on
the ship. It wasn't the kind of ship for masked balls, but Miss
Tone felt a masked ball should always be given the night
before landing. She was the only female beachcomber I

ever got to know very well and she had all the faults and the few virtues of beachcombers.

"But a masked ball on a freight boat carrying a dozen passengers," Mike protested.

"We're human, aren't we?"

"This is true, but . . ."

"Then it's a masked ball."

There was nothing for it but to have the masked ball.

It was a fine party. Miss Tone danced the cancan on the captain's table and a sailor fell overboard but was recovered, and two men woke up the next day wondering if they had really promised Miss Tone they would marry her. She was hunting for some younger man ("What the hell, kid, so I like to mother 'em"). Mike was amused and cynical.

We coasted along past Point Deminical, and Point Judas, and at last we could feel the tides of the Gulf of Nicoya lift us, and the lights of San José marked the horizon. Mike and I were standing on deck watching the colors of the New World. It is odd, but the Americas *do* look different from any place else. Nowhere else is that shade of green, that mountain ridge behind it; the sun seems to have a polished shine; and no matter where they put you down in the Americas you know *this* is the New World. Columbus must have seen lots of it like this: a scribble of green feathers against a chalk-blue sky, the shape of trees on a low shore, and then a wild salad of lofting tropical hills.

Miss Tone appeared at my elbow and leaned over the rail. She looked, in the strong sunlight, like a gypsy. Mike pointed out the shore and the city. "It's a great place. They eat six times a day. Their cigars are very good but flavored with vanilla."

"You're kidding a country girl," she said.

"No. They have more flowers than any other country in

the world and their eggplant, *berenjena con tomate,* is the only way to make the dish."

"I'm going to get some camera shots of one of the oxcart parades."

"They have good ones."

PORT SAN JOSÉ

"Good. I need a good fortuneteller . . . King is behind with his letters."

King was Miss Tone's soothsayer in New Orleans. He wrote her a weekly letter explaining how out of his "voices" had come a feeling for her and she was to follow his instructions.

"Yes," said Miss Tone, "I must find a fortuneteller to fill in the missing orders from King."

We went ashore just after breakfast and Miss Tone and I saw Mike off in the plane. We all shook hands and said, "We'll be in touch."

THE FORTUNETELLER OF SAN JOSÉ

At the hotel we had to have another breakfast of coffee, fruit, and some little tortillas, and at ten we had the second breakfast (it was bad manners to refuse), this one with sweet buns and more fruit. Lunch came at twelve, just a bit of tortillas, frijoles, rice, eggs, soup, and meatballs, and wonderful vegetables.

Miss Tone looked at me and wiped the effort of eating off her face. "I can't take any more."

"There *is* a two o'clock lunch."

"Take me out of here. My scar tissue is going to pop."

THE FORTUNETELLER OF SAN JOSÉ

I hired a car and we bumped over muddy roads and around oxen and donkeys eating and went to look for a fortuneteller. We found him in an inn called the Royal Palm. A moody man with bangs in his face smoking a small vanilla-flavored cigar and drinking the native *chicha*, mixed with *aguardiente* —local brandy that is powerful enough to run jet planes. He invited us to have the two-o'clock meal with him. Just some chocolate, little cakes, and more *chicha*, this time flavored with pineapple.

He looked at Miss Tone and said, "I have a feeling you are a child of the occult. Great things will happen to you here."

"Just what? King says I vibrate to unknown forces. Sometimes he calls me and says he has a feeling I need help. I always do."

The fortuneteller nodded and took the two ten-dollar bills from Miss Tone's fingers. "He is a wise man. I would kiss him were he here. I, too, have a feeling."

"You're just like King!"

"You love youth, you love the tender green things."

"You're *just* like King."

But it was time for the afternoon *antipasto*, a cocktail, and again the fruit. We left the inn feeling heavy and Miss Tone was full of magic.

"I'm a slob, but I like it."

"Aren't you ashamed—a grown woman going to these windbags?"

"Stevie, don't ever be born a woman."

I had no answer for that one.

We got back just in time for *la sopa*, a puréed broth— they shoot people if they miss it. Also *mero*, bass, and *salpicón*, which is meat with mustard greens. We did gamely by it.

STILL EATING

Of course, at six we sat down to dinner: *fricasé de gallina de guinea*, fricaseed fowl and rice; *chayote*, a sort of alligator pear; and a dessert of *dulce de higos con leche de coco*, ripe figs with coconuts.

Miss Tone groaned, "I feel myself tearing apart. Better get me some needle and thread."·

The waiter smiled. "At nine we open the ox pit . . . roast steer."

"Let me out of here," said Miss Tone.

I took her to her room and bathed her brow and said she needn't worry, I was sure they had a stomach pump in town.

"Don't leave me. I want to die with my friends around me."

I sat down by the window and lit one of the native cigars. Miss Tone tossed on the bed and grew quiet, and she lay there staring at the ceiling where a lovenest of wasps were busy making brown-paper houses.

"I always destroy my happiness. I ruined my work, I got tossed out of all the studios. The will for ruin is mine—lots of people have it."

"It's just the food. You'll be all right in the morning."

"I had a brain and I had a body, now everyone is sorry for me."

"I'm not." I poured out two small glasses of *aguardiente* and we drank and I left her looking at the wasps and went down into the streets. It was a gay night in town, and they were dancing in the inns and walking around the parks. The young men walked one way, the young girls the other, and when a young man saw someone he liked he went up to her, tipped his hat, and the couple walked off into the park arm in arm. It was a local custom and very nice. I got back to the hotel for the midnight snack, some good beef and *ostras*, oysters, and *sopa de fideos*.

I slept well and got up the next morning and set up my camera and got some good ox-wagon scenes and the natives in holiday dress. Miss Tone was up and sitting in the sun in a gay sunsuit.

"Feeling any pain?" I asked.

"Feeling nothing. The fortuneteller is ten minutes late."

"These Latin countries—they laugh at time."

"I'm going to Mexico—do a picture story for *Look*."

I took her to a gambling house where we lost enough money to make us welcome and then we rode in the hired car among the lemon groves in blossom. Back at the hotel they were serving meal five of the day, but the fortuneteller was waiting for Miss Tone.

"Something came to me. I had to come right over. I am worried."

Miss Tone beamed, "I knew it. I knew today had something the matter with it."

The fortuneteller looked over the dining room. "But first let us eat."

I wanted to say no, but Miss Tone never crossed a soothsayer yet so we went in and had a baked *jamón,* ham, and haddock, Spanish style, small stuffed squashes called *calabacitos rellenos,* and bananas cooked in sherry.

The fortuneteller wiped his lips and sighed. "You should have been here before the war. The food was grand. Now they throw this at you. Still, man must eat, and all flesh is grass in the end, eh?"

Miss Tone said, "I don't feel well."

The fortuneteller took her hand and removed a ten-dollar bill from it. "I have studied and I have prayed and I have consulted old books of the occult. There is in you a hollowness."

"*Not* now!"

"There is in you a void. Something needs to fill you. I

see for you a period of waiting and then, yes, you will again
be what you once were."

"A successful cameraman?"

"No, a married woman."

Miss Tone groaned. "You mean I have to go through all
that again!"

She wasn't feeling well so I decided to get her back on
the boat. We left the fortuneteller nibbling on some pork
loin . . . and we got on the boat.

NORTH ON THE PACIFIC

The next few days we went north past Nicaragua and the
Gulf of Fonseca. Miss Tone did not go ashore at Choluteca in
Honduras.

"I've decided to settle down. No more the crackpot, the
damn fool patsy for every mad setup; just a little old lady
living in peace of mind."

"Good. The second mate has a cat. Settle down and start
some knitting. I'm going ashore."

When I came back I found Miss Tone in the bar. She was
playing draw-poker with the engine-room gang and smoking
one of my Costa Rica cigars . . . a fist full of aces.

She grinned. "Life in the old crow yet. Just got a letter
forwarded from King. He says I'll be hot at Luce publications
soon."

I was on deck when she came out later with two balloons
of brandy and handed me one.

It was cool on deck, the wide Pacific was colored deep
green, the sky was hung with silver stars, almost low enough
to bite. From the shore came the green smell of sleeping jungle and the sense of growing plants and trees. We stood at
the rail and the moon came out, and in the bar they were talking loud. In the salon someone started the record player and

they were dancing a *samba*. On the bridge the captain walked
back and forth exercising his little fat dog. A bell rang, the
white wake trailed behind, and in a few days we would be in
Mexico. The smell of blossoms came strongly from the shore.
Miss Tone stood on the rail looking shoreward.

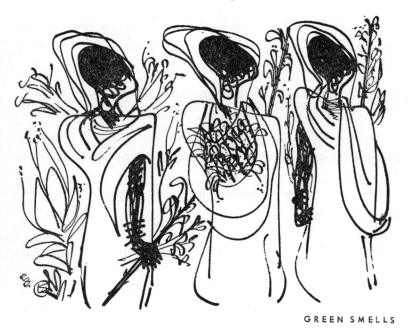

GREEN SMELLS

27   modern Aztecs

I WANTED to get to Mexico City in time for the season
—the *fiesta de toros* and maybe nab a ticket among the *delantera de tendido,* among the better seats. I don't get as excited
as Mr. Hemingway over bullfighting, but when it's a good
day and the bulls aren't *malo* (lousy), it's a fine sight and
lots of color and fun—except for the bull, of course, who ends
up as a *mole de olla,* a very fine dish of beef and string beans
with a hot pepper sauce—hotter than the gates of Hell.

I was staying with friends in a small white house of fifty
rooms and six baths (two of which worked) when the phone
rang and it was Miss Tone.

"Hello," I said, "aren't you too innocent for a Mexico City winter?"

"Hold on to your hat. You're going to a wedding."

"Whose?"

"Don't tremble, Stevie . . . it's a British gentleman from the West Indies. Veddy, veddy British. Getting hitched this afternoon. Fifth time for me."

HOTEL LIFE—MEXICO

"You're forgetting that beach bum who ate himself to death."

"He didn't die—I mislaid him. Come on over, you're giving the bride away."

I decided I'd rather give this bride away than keep her.

The bride was dressing when I got to her hotel. I was very fond of Miss Tone and I hoped this wedding would last longer than most of her desires to go domestic.

She was crawling into her wedding gown and I helped pin

it up. She had tried out a new hair dye, and her silver fingernails had been tinted the color of old silver dollars and she
seemed game enough to carry on.

"Wait till you meet Cedric. He's something."

"Just what is that?" I asked.

"Some fancy breed of Englishman, planter and all that.
My dress on straight?"

"Yes, but your hips aren't."

"These damn girdles. Buy me a lunch. I'm due at the Embassy for the wedding at four."

In broad daylight, Miss Tone in war paint was splendid.
I figured in Mexico City the people are used to *everything*,
and I took her to a small eating place where it grew dark
early.

We had *mole de guajolote,* which is a pepper sauce
and turkey that is the best way to eat turkey, no matter what
they say in New England. And a soup, *caldo de pollo con
aquacate;* also *cuauhtemoc,* eggs with black beans. We drank
pulque, made of pomegranate juice, and when Miss Tone
wanted to celebrate we had the native *tequila* that kicks with
all four hoofs at once.

Miss Tone tossed off her shoes and sat back in her new
girdle. "What was I looking for, Stevie . . . in those days?"

"The same as usual," I said, motioning the waiter to us.
"We better get to that wedding."

"I always feel sad as a bride. You'd think just because
it's a habit I'd get used to it. But it always gets me right
here."

"That's the *tequila.*"

FRIEND OF THE BRIDE

The Embassy was closed, the wedding was to be held in a
little chapel off a side street and I met the bridegroom, a lit-

tle chocolate-colored chap with a little old mother who sneered at what I later found out she called us—"Colonials."

Cedric didn't look very English, more Hindu I thought, but he had a thick Oxford accent and a clipped way of talking and I hoped they would be very happy.

I said to Miss Tone, "Pretty dark for an Englishman, isn't he?"

"Always out in the sun keeping the natives busy on the plantation, you know."

I nodded and was very sad through it all, thinking how much fun Miss Tone had been on the world tour, and how it was all so sad in this peeling chapel, with Cedric's mother weeping because she was losing her baby and because she had a bad cold and because the place smelled of garlic drying in the rafters. After the wedding we all went and had white wine and red wine, rather above room temperature, and ate little cakes made of *chimaja* root and anise seeds.

"Where is the honeymoon?" I asked Miss Tone.

"Cedric's mother's place . . . a villa outside of town."

"The best of luck," I said, and I bravely kissed her in the middle of the melting make-up and gripped her arm as if to say: "Courage, fellow world traveler . . ." But out loud, I didn't say anything. I got a cab to the bullfight ring where my friends were waiting for me. They had just killed the third bull and the *aficionados* were tossing cushions onto the heads of the sword holders behind the red *barrera* that kept the bulls in the ring.

FIESTA DE TOROS

It was a very good afternoon. The *picador* on his sad little horse was very good, and the horse was padded like a Yale fullback so he didn't get hurt—much. Next, the *banderillas* were placed very close in the bull's back and he charged close

MOTHER OF THE BRIDEGROOM

—*ceñido* it's called, and the fighter in his tight-fitting *tale-quillas* seemed scared (as who wouldn't be), but he made the cape passes well. I knew enough to know a *camboi* from a pass *a rodillas*, but he lost me after that. The short *veronica* pass is almost as good as ballet, but the crowd didn't like this guy and they called him *hi de puta*, howled *fuera* and called him *mamarracho* (stumble-bum).

My friends asked where I had been and I said a wedding. "American?"

"Los Angeles type," I said. "Once to Reno, and twice to the dogs, and now lonely and worried she is getting old."

"Very sad. Why do all American women marry so badly?"

"There must be fifty million who don't," I said.

"But they age so quickly and try so hard to look young, and drink the highballs and take the sleeping pills. No, it's a bad way of life American women have. And living like men in bars and fast cars and being picked up and taken to tango places."

"They love to dance."

"They are a sad lot. And so skinny. Like making love to a boy."

"Hips are coming back."

"Very sad, American women. Let us watch the bull. It's the kill."

The fighter took the sword from his *ayudante* and the

mob yelped *anda, anda!* The bull hooked left and tore open
the ornate jacket. The baited animal charged again and now
the riffraff and the *delantera de tendido* all shouted as one.
The fighter made a *chicuelinas* with his cape and hunted the
small spot between the bull's shoulders, for this is the only
place to kill a bull. He hit the bone, the horns got him in the
side, and he was lifted and tossed. The *picadores* went in on
their horses, and his *cuadrilla* used their capes to draw the
bull away. The fighter stood up, holding himself in, and got
el toro with a swift push of the sword. The little mules with
bells on their legs dragged out the bull and the bullring doc‧
tor got the fighter, and we drank *cerveza*, the native beer,
and said it had been a very fine *fiesta de toros* indeed.

We went to dinner to the Hotel Del Prado. We had rice
with shrimp, and a cake called *rosca de reyes* which as far
as I could ever make out is fruit in liqueurs. I could taste in it
cognac, Cointreau, fresh pineapple, bananas, strawberries,
almonds, oranges, cherries, and apples. It is served chilled
and on beds of ice.

STUDY OF A NATION

"Por la luna doy un peso, por el sol doy un tostón"
(For the moon I'd give a peso, for the sun I'll give half.)
. . . sings the man at the street corner . . .

The idea that Mexico is a paradox is nonsense. It's a nation that is not hard to understand if one wants to—a place
that has a great deal of everything, including what the intel-
lectuals, the businessmen, the moralists, and the ritualists
want to find. It's also a damn fine place from the Sierra Madre
down to Guatemala. It's dusty, wet, empty, jungle-mad, full
of flowers, trees, the palm, the *henequén* . . . all the *tierra
caliente* (hot lands) and the *tierra templada* (the uplands).
And plenty of bull fights . . .

It's a corn culture, tempered by cotton and beans and bananas. Coffee, cocoa beans, cactus, and coyotes are its life too. And if you like volcanoes they have them hot and cold. So much that is foolish has been said about Mexico that even knowing the country, one still thinks of it in terms of armadillos and mahogany. But the people are alive and stirring, the faces from the Toltec carving are still alive, their villages sit near the pyramids of the Sun and Moon at Teotihuacán (the spelling is back-breaking). Their art forms are as old as Egypt, geometric and squat in the most fashionable of modern form, crossed with Marx and Quetzalcoatl, mad monks, plumed snakes, and tigers.

QUIÉN SABÉ?

There is so much to see. To do. To cut a way into the jungle in Yucatán. To see Chichen Itza, that great Mayan ruin, is to make us in the U.S.A. feel only six weeks old. I like best the figure of Chac Mool, the Red Claw, a Mayan king who was a popular art object, resting on the ground in the shape of a half-moon and on his lap that altar for human sacrifice; for sinister rituals have taken place in a land of overdramatic skies and fearful landscapes.

The feeble present has lost out in Mexico, one feels. It is again becoming a pre-Cortez world, again an Indian-and-corn culture reverting to its place, so that even in the catacombs of Guanajuato, the dead are becoming more modern in that return of a country, free of its Spanish and monkish grabbing, to something stark and beautiful.

The world of *mañana; ¿Quién sabe?* and *¿Qué importa?* for all its fish-tailed Caddys and iceboxes and TV and machine guns, is truly pagan—fully pagan when it eats its skulls made of cake on *Día de los Muertos,* the Day of the Dead or All Saints' Day, when its priests make smoke, incense, prayer and create no passion. Where the people's rationalism and skepticism are mixed with Marx into something unknown to that founding father of present-day trouble.

STREET SCENE

I liked to walk from the Hotel Del Prado, very swank and up to date, to the Paseo de la Reforma, as fashionable as Fifth Avenue, and see men who have never worn shoes and women who think girdles a torture weapon of the church. It is not that progress has stopped here, but that Mexico may yet detour around the pragmatism of having everything and knowing nothing. Emerson would understand them. He said, "Everything has two handles, beware which one you pick up."

The corner singer croons:

> *"La cucaracha, la cucaracha,*
> *Ya no puede caminar*
> *Porque no tiene, porque le falta,*
> *Marijuana que fumar.*
>
> The cockroach, the cockroach,
> Can no longer walk
> Because it's got no—got no
> Marijuana to smoke."

I walked a long time to clear my head.

The next evening we all went to a night club and then to an art show. Some place near morning, I got back to my friends' house and fell asleep and it seemed I slept for a few days. But that wasn't true because I was to lecture at the big art school that afternoon. I made it, poked a lot of fun at clown painters, and said a few things that Picasso had once said. I approved of their great artists and hoped we could steal a few. I was in the hall later, looking at the students' work, when they came and said I was wanted on the phone.

It was Cedric, the bridegroom, and he sounded very British, as if they had sunk a battleship or lost London.

"My wife left me. Have you any idea?"

"Of what?"

"Where she is?"

"None at all. What broke it up?"

"The mater is a bit of a Tartar, you know . . . insisted on sleeping in the next room. You know these Mexican walls. Upset my wife no end. Fearful row. Mater said some hard things about Colonials, you know, and my wife called us 'sunburnt field hands' and left. In her nightgown."

"That's warmer than her evening gowns."

"You will try and find her, old boy?"

"No," I said. "I stopped holding her head a long time ago."

"But you're a dear friend of hers."

"Look," I said, "when she stops bouncing I may brush her off."

"You're a bounder!" said Cedric, hanging up, and of course he was right, but I hadn't come to Mexico to ride herd on Miss Tone. Besides, like all beachcombers, Miss Tone had a way of never doing anything fatal.

I spent the evening with my friends proving I couldn't gamble against the local wheels, and as they were going to a late mass, I decided to go see a movie. The only thing I hadn't seen in town was an old Warner Brothers epic, about soiled love among the rich and the suffering of a girl, played by Bette Davis (or was it Joan Crawford?) who had everything, but *still* was unhappy.

It wasn't a very good movie and the place wasn't crowded . . . and then I heard someone sniffing and someone said, "Can I borrow your g.d. handkerchief?" It was Miss Tone.

She blew and wiped and groaned and snorted and handed me back the damp linen and a limp, clawlike hand.

"Isn't it lousy!" she said. "Something I saw years ago, and now when I need it, *there* it is! Nothing is ever lost, Stevie. We wall it up but it weeps in the walls. The cables are always there, aren't they . . . the thing is in our veins, isn't it?"

We sat there looking at the soggy epic and Miss Tone cheered up and played every scene with the woman on the screen. When a juicy bit of dialogue appeared she repeated it in my ear and her silvered claws dug into my hand. It was a pretty bad picture.

A GOOD-BY

Later she repaired her face in the ladies' room and I walked her back to her hotel.

"Don't tell me," she said, "I know it's all my fault. And why? I'm a sappy romantic. I believe in love, in human kindness, in honor and faith."

"Sure you do."

"Oh, I slip, I know that. But I'm not hard, I'm not evil, and I'm not emotionless. That's my crime in a world gone hard and cruel. There isn't room for the things I believe in. The softer emotions, the kinder ways of life."

"Sure," I recited. "You're valuable, you're a museum piece."

Miss Tone laughed. "Sorry I slopped over. What difference does it make? It's all just a little more emotional scar tissue, a little more I can be sorry for when I can't sleep, when I'm lonely, when I wonder why the sleeping pills don't work. Buy you a drink, Mister?"

"After I buy you some food. You eaten today?"

"No. Let's have a big meal and drink to going home— U.S.A. If I had a flag I'd wave it."

I knew what she meant. It was going to be good getting home. I had been away a long, long time. I was going home to the kids, the family, the big house, the old books, the loved pictures, my friends.

I decided to buy Miss Tone a pair of lovebirds—they were portable and hearty, and she could recite her dialogue to them and they wouldn't talk back, but just whistle at her— and Miss Tone always liked to be whistled at.

HOME

When I got home, the olive trees of Beverly Hills were dropping their violet fruit on the landscaped lawn and the kids looked bigger, and the family more beautiful. It was good to be home. Banal words I suppose, but I liked looking over the blue painted walls of the house and the remembered

shapes of the furniture, the bindings of the books, the slashing
surfaces of the paintings, the green of the garden. Our cat,
Red Prince, rubbed against my shoes that had seen India and
China and the African plain. I wondered if he smelled lions,
machine gunners, and holy men, head-hunters, black mar-
keteers, and tea drinkers, dance-hall girls, bushboys, graft-
ers, and elephants . . .

HOME

a kind of epilogue

**"NO ONE OF US CAN FORBID
THE FUTURE"**

inscription on a monument

IN THE morning the rest of the world seems far away.
The colors are different—there is a special kind of yellow.
Yellow is the color of the coastal plains and the forgotten
farms and the shoulders of the old highways. It is an American yellow. It is not the brisk yellow of the drinks in the
cafés in Rome. It is not the mad, hot yellow of Van Gogh
carving up French fields and tablecloths into patterns of his
own. It is not the varnished yellows of the old masters, nor

298

the now-tired yellows of the wild young men of 1910. This is
the yellow of a new world in a brisk sun. A yellow on the
wheat fields and the milk sheds and the town and station
wagons of the farmer who has saved a buck. It's the yellow
of dead palm fronds, the yellow of curb markings, the yellow
of a young girl's hair waiting for a corn-colored bus. It's
suddenly to me a million shades of the same color; and when
the dusk comes, it dies away to soft green and blues, and into
icy purples, but morning will find it again the same damn
shade of yellow, the same strong tones of American yellow . . .

THE SEARCH

But I wanted to know if the world had seemed better in
the past. Have the American artists caught any of its "just-
gone past?" Can it be examined close up—honestly?

No. Far from the great School of Paris are the hills of
home, and the svelte line of Braque does not often whirl over
Frisco. There is no abstract formula in the Dust Bowl, and the
orange trees and the big rivers rolling to the sea do not speak
to stones in the tones of Dali.

This is the American ground as it had been since the Little
Big Horn, I felt, when the buffalo grass grew wild and the
Redcoats marched out at Yorktown singing, "The World
Turned Upside Down." Lee, who was born in the age of Manet,
never saw a Renoir or took Toulouse-Lautrec in as a house
guest. There are little farms under the black murder of summer storms that lack the shapes of Miro, and the Fresno fruit
is never the color of Bonnard's. Somehow we have become
lost in strangers' art forms. We have gone far down an alley
of bright European tones and clashing Continental shapes,
and every Main Street has its fly-specked cubist, its swamp-

AVANT-GARDE

water Dufy, the color and markings borrowed from Modigliani. The good sins of Cézanne sit on the shoulders of talented sign painters in Vermont, and Matisse waltzes in the heart of every ladylike decorator, when drunk, in living rooms in Beverly Hills and West Lung, Nevada, and Great Neck and Troy, New York.

No. There was no answer in art. I would try someone who could do it with words.

THE SEARCH CONTINUED

I went to see an old teacher of mine called Sam. He sat by his fireplace, a drink in his hand. The old man grinned.

"You want to see things beyond the call of sanity, duty, or filling a belly, and all the nonsense they make an education with. How did the world look to you?"

"I'm just a traveler."

The old man relaxed slowly, fitting his tired body, his aching bone and marrow, into a more comfortable position. "The trouble with human beings is they don't come to a way of thinking early enough. Ever read Pyrrho? One of the wise old Greek duffers . . . had a philosophy of skepticism. You listening?"

"I'm all ears."

"He broke life down to a set of reasons for living that weren't too bad. When I was young I liked them. 'Certainty,' he said, 'is unattainable.' If you're smart you'll suspend most final judgments and look for tranquility rather than truth that changes every time you see it. All theories are most likely wrong some place, so don't let the legends and conventions of your time bother you, he taught. The sense and reason can't ever give us true knowledge . . . You see, our senses distort the object in seeing it, and reason—hell, reason is merely the lousy sophist servant of desire. Get it?"

"I'm listening."

"What is an experience? he asked. The same one may please one man and disgust the next . . . according to circumstance or mood. Remember, the same object may be small or ugly, evil or good, stupid or beautiful, according to where we live or where we stand. Everything is only opinion, nothing is ever quite true. Don't envy the future or the past. All desire is a delusion, you learn in time, but keep plenty of desires on hand. They're fun—not bad if not overdone. Life is an uncertain good, death not a certain evil. Best of all is a calm acceptance, bear all with proud patience . . . Try is all we can do. The bloodstream pumps for our groin *and* head, and we are excited by a naked body or a colored sky or a big meal or a bottle of brandy. Live life in clean beds, paint, read, eat, and keep your mind and eyes open."

"You ought to be a critic."

"The best critic is always fifty years behind anything he looks at. The rest a hundred years. Early in this century, we saw clearer."

THE PAST JOINS THE PRESENT

Sam stirred the embers together and looked off toward sounds in the night.

"Was it like this in Europe in 1910, Sam?"

The old man turned over on his back and his eyes looked up at the stars outside the windows. "1910—London, Paris, Rome . . . Montmartre and Clichy. A bunch of wild kids in rioting flats and cold studios crazy over the new forms, new words, new music. Nigger carving and line drawings out of Asia and the bloodstained war shield of the South Sea Islanders, *Souvenirs du Quartier Latin.* And the first hints from Freud and Joyce. There was a new inside life of dreams and symbols that could be felt . . . maybe. How young the world was, and how we howled on our hind legs and painted and wrote stuff that popped the critics' eyes out on stems. That was a time and a moment, and we turned the whole world of culture and art on its head. Maybe we did it all wrong, and the whole modern movement is now tired and silly, but it wasn't like that then. You could still buy a Cézanne under a hundred bucks, discover Shaw, respect Debussy, and all the girls were fat and beautiful in the *cabaret artistique,* even if they didn't bathe much. We turned our backs on the whole daffy history of the past and invented a new era every night at dinner. Picasso was a thin, black-eyed kid, and I remember

the old men with tired faces . . . Mark Twain behind a big
cigar, Degas full of witty bile, his Wassermann as high as his
I.Q.—blind as a hoot owl in the daylight. Woodrow Wilson
teaching history. And Renoir, the brushes strapped to his
crippled hands, painting the pink human buttocks into art.
Stravinsky's music shocking the fools. The crazy, wonderful
Jew boys, Modigliani, Soutine, and Chagall. Matisse scared
as a peasant of his wife, and the old, old Lautrec posters, fragments of them still on the walls the people stopped to urinate
against. *Mon vieux* Aristide Bruant singing: *"Quand j'vois
filles de dix-sept ans . . ."* We Americans, Weber and Leo
Stein, Henry James, the old J. P. Morgan. And the others who
once in a while got a check from home . . . the cattle millionaires, gypsy fiddlers, Gibson girls . . . O'Henry's short
stories and the last of the great piano players. And all the
nights we slept in each other's studios on the rue Caulaincourt
to keep warm, and the spring when the plumbing worked again
and the chestnut trees, those goddamn chestnut trees out of
bad popular fiction, got green with color and all the streets
looked as if Pissarro had just finished painting them . . .
Only art, cultures, forms, mattered . . . Others could have
the money and the big houses and the wars and the family
life . . . we were dedicated . . . we . . . Max, Yvette,
Mari R. London or the Jardin de Paree . . . There was a
cobalt blue over the river bookstalls . . . down with the
salon . . . and the *Ecole des Beaux Arts* . . . Up Bonnard
and Le Figaro . . . We had a good world. And didn't know
it . . ."

The old man, his big face carved by the fire into something
powerful—and yet tragic too, for the force, the strength, was
going now. The old man would be older very soon. The skull
was thrusting its way out of the weathered flesh, the bite of
time was digging deeper.

The fire dancing on the old lined face suggested all that had happened once . . .

I went home to my house, to my family.

The traveler had returned again.

DESIRE